In *Lessons from Grace*, Uma Girish offers us simple reflections from everyday life that are guaranteed to deepen our compassion for ourselves and others. Girish gives us new jewels that hold the power of sweetness and joy.

— **Janet Conner**
author of *Writing Down Your Soul: How to Activate and Listen to the Extraordinary Voice Within*

Lessons from Grace contains powerful and valuable truths that lead you on a transformational journey of living in the moment with freedom, joy, and true happiness. Thought-provoking, it inspires the reader to live the life of their dreams with passion, honesty, and fearlessness.

— **Anita Moorjani**
New York Times bestselling author of *Dying to Be Me: My Journey from Cancer, to Near Death, to True Healing*

It's one thing to care for a baby as a new mother and it's quite another to unexpectedly care for one in a later season in life. Uma Girish's mindful memoir evokes the wisdom and beauty of a small child experiencing the world for the first time. What might our lives be like if we honour our natural states of being, full of curiosity, readiness to learn, and present-moment awareness? This lovely book is full of reminders on how to cultivate safety, nourishment, adventure, and, perhaps, mostly keenly, how to rest in loving awareness of our own humanity.

— **Tara Cousineau, PhD**
author of *The Kindness Cure: How the Science of Compassion Can Heal Your Heart and Your World*

Lessons from Grace: What a Baby Taught Me about Living and Loving is a moving meditation on the essence of life. Told through the author's experiences with a baby, the short and sweet essays make us pause and reflect on the essentials of life. Poignant, contemplative, humorous, and profound at the same time, this is a book you will return to for its timeless wisdom and wonder.

— Christine Wheeler
EFT Tapping Expert and author of *The Tapping Solution for Teenage Girls: How to Stop Freaking Out and Keep Being Awesome*

LESSONS FROM GRACE

What a Baby Taught Me about
Living and Loving

Uma Girish

HAY HOUSE

Carlsbad, California • New York City
London • Sydney • New Delhi

Copyright © 2019 Uma Girish

Published in the United States by: Hay House, Inc.: www.hayhouse.com*
Published in Australia by: Hay House Australia Pty. Ltd.: www.hayhouse.com.au
Published in the United Kingdom by: Hay House UK, Ltd.: www.hayhouse.co.uk
Published in India by: Hay House Publishers India: www.hayhouse.co.in

ISBN: 978-93-86832-81-8
e-Book ISBN: 978-93-86832-87-0

Printed in the United States of America

'When "true self" is the topic, children are the best source, because they live so close to their birthright gifts . . . In my granddaughter I actually observed something I could once take only on faith: we are born with a seed of selfhood that contains the spiritual DNA of our uniqueness—an encoded birthright knowledge of who we are, why we are here, and how we are related to others.'

— Parker J. Palmer,
*A Hidden Wholeness: The Journey Toward
an Undivided Life*

Dear Grace,
Our hearts are knitted together forever.

CONTENTS

PREFACE

When Chris, an aspiring memoirist, joined our writers' group one Saturday morning in 2009, I didn't have the faintest clue that our lives would weave together in unimaginable ways.

Chris was funny, warm, caring, and easy to like. Soon, the two of us became fast friends. A few months later, he introduced me to his girlfriend, Tiffany. There was a kindness and sweetness to her that I found endearing.

I know now that we were drawn together in ways that only the Universe can orchestrate. When people are meant to come together for certain reasons, they just do. Game nights and soulful conversations bonded us over time.

Late one evening, my daughter and I were watching the tail end of the Oscars when Chris called.

'I just proposed,' he said, sounding a little breathless.

'Wow, congratulations! That is awesome news!' I shouted, as my daughter looked at me with questions in her eyes.

Chris' next words touched me deeply. 'You're the first one to know, so . . . nothing on Facebook yet, okay?'

My family and I drove to their beautiful October wedding in 2011, a day that will be specially remembered for the two canine ring bearers, Emily and Teddy.

Many months later, a teacher explained to me that every encounter is a holy encounter. In that moment, it made complete sense. Chris walking to our writer's table as we pondered plot lines and punctuation, was definitely one such holy encounter.

Around this time, I was mentoring with Randy, a church-going Christian, whose heart was big enough to support a Hindu. I was working through my grief following my mother's sudden death in early 2009. To better understand my grieving heart and connect with the truth of my life experiences, Randy had me pick a series of books which we read together. We connected the themes of these books with my own journey.

At the time, we were reading *The Prayer of Jabez: Breaking Through to the Blessed Life* where the author, Bruce Wilkinson, shares the story of a little-known Biblical character, Jabez, who wants nothing more than to serve God. But Jabez is the runt of the litter in human terms and his large ambitions to serve God and make a difference in the world are laughable. However, by channelling God's power and honouring His timeline to increase his sphere of influence, Jabez goes on to have a tremendous impact on the history of Israel.

Bruce Wilkinson shares his own Jabez act in the book. He tells the story of walking into a cafe one morning and letting God know that he is willing to serve someone, anyone. He simply wishes to be used by his Creator. Moments later, a couple walks into the cafe and starts a casual conversation with him which turns out to be life-changing for all three. The couple share that they are headed for a separation and Bruce ends up being the cosmic agent of change who reverses their destiny.

Through this incident, Bruce reinforces the truth that only by relying on God can anyone achieve the seemingly impossible; in this case, repair a relationship headed for the rocks. The story ends on a cheerful note. The couple leave the cafe determined to give their marriage another chance.

Inspired by Jabez and Bruce, I resolved to have my own God moment. I don't know what I was thinking, but there I was, sitting in a Starbucks one Saturday morning, trying to imitate a biblical, world-renowned Christian teacher. I made a bargain with God to send me someone to serve, and if He did, I would keep my promise. I tried to make conscious eye contact with everyone who stepped into the coffee shop, wondering who was meant for me. No one even glanced my way. Forty minutes later I went home, discouraged and despondent.

An hour later, Chris called.

'Are you going to be home this evening?' he sounded serious. 'Tiff and I would like to come talk to you about something important,' he said.

'Sure,' I replied. 'I'm not doing much.'

They had been married for only two weeks, so I was a bit perplexed, and thought to myself, *Trouble in paradise already?*

My chance at a life-changing conversation presented itself hours later when Chris and Tiffany walked through my front door. As they settled down on the couch, I sensed the tension in the air. Chris dove into it without any preamble, 'Tiff is pregnant!'

A tiny speck of life had miraculously overpowered all the preventive measures the couple had taken. This soul, uncaring of anyone else's control issues, or preferences, knew its perfect timing. Confused and anxious at this unexpected turn of events, the couple was seeking some degree of clarity on how to proceed.

I don't remember much of what was said, but I distinctly recall the words I spoke to them, 'This is out of your hands. This baby wants to be born.'

In that moment, I hadn't the slightest clue how that one conversation was going to profoundly impact and change *all* our lives. When Chris and Tiffany left a couple of hours later, they were holding hands and breathing easier.

As I look back, I know that my life and their lives were part of a giant tapestry that started to weave together that very moment.

***

Baby Grace arrived on a balmy May afternoon. I was sitting in the audience at Harpo Studios for a taping of the *Oprah's Lifeclass* show, a seminal moment for a die-hard Oprah fan from India, when I received the news.

It was the day after the show that I held Grace for the very first time. I was mesmerised by her perfection and whispered a welcome.

A few days later, Chris called me from work. I sensed the urgency in his voice when he asked, 'Can you go over to my house and hold the baby? Tiff is in a lot of pain today.'

Tiffany's muscles and joints had been causing her a lot of pain right through the pregnancy which continued even after the baby arrived.

I was at their place within a few minutes. I held Grace for almost two hours, feeling an unspeakable love for this baby as she slept blissfully in my arms.

'She is so calm in your arms,' Tiffany remarked.

I continued my baby visits, marvelling at Grace's perfect features and contemplating the miracle of life. I felt a soul-level connection with this baby in the deepest part of my being, something I had no words for and didn't know how to explain.

***

A phone call from Tiffany on a July evening was no surprise, but her request certainly was.

'We would love for you to be Grace's nanny,' she said.

I gulped.

Tiffany and Chris were now two-month-old parents. Tiffany was running out of maternity leave and had to return to full-time work.

We had known each other for about two years now. It made sense that they were considering someone they liked and trusted to care for their baby girl while they were away. They also knew that my husband was paying a significant tuition bill for our daughter's college education, and I was out of a job and nurturing a fledgling business. A second income would certainly help. When Chris told me that they wanted someone with good and calm energy to watch their baby, I was deeply touched.

As the pros and cons of a possible decision began whirling inside my head, Tiffany's soft voice filled the phone line with details—my hours, the pay, and my preferred babysitting location (their house or mine).

I had about fifteen hours to let them know my decision. The clock was ticking, and if I turned down the offer, they would ask another friend.

My child-rearing years were a distant memory and far behind me. My daughter was a sophomore in college, and I was focused on writing and doing everything I could to get my books out into the world. I was committed to my vision of supporting grieving women and teaching workshops. A part-time nanny job was nowhere on my horizon.

And yet, from all that I have learned, I know that there are no accidents in an intelligent Universe. I drifted off to sleep that night whispering the words, 'Please, God! Give me a sign . . . tell me. Is this what I'm meant to do at this time in my life?'

Sleep eluded me; I tossed and turned, the sheets twisting with my anxiety. I imagined myself with a wet burp rag on my shoulder, a colicky baby screaming her lungs out as I rocked and soothed her, but to no avail. Was my life coming a full-circle moment with poopy diapers and spit-up milk? The images of my future were fast receding—an ecstatic audience of book lovers eager for more of my work, book-signing sessions, interviews, and Oprah's couch . . . everything was fading.

Through the fitful sleep of that night, I had a dream. In that dream, I saw my parents' (who had passed) smiling faces and felt the tenderness of their gaze. The next morning, I woke up with these words in my head: 'It is God's grace.'

God's grace? What was that supposed to mean? My sleep-fuddled mind was still warming up. And, then, all of a sudden, everything rushed in—Tiffany's call, my confusion, subsequent request for divine guidance, and the dream.

And now, this message—It is God's grace.

To me, grace is the gift that God bestows upon us. It seeks and finds us when we are ready and willing to receive.

I sat up in my bed, beginning to stitch it all together. The baby's name was Grace.

There was no doubt in my mind anymore; this was divine guidance. I didn't understand how this whole nanny commitment would unfold, but I knew that answers would arrive, piece by piece. I needed to climb a single step at a time, even if I couldn't see the whole staircase.

The next morning, I called Tiffany and said yes. I also told her that I would watch Grace at their place. After all, we lived less than two miles from each other, and I simply didn't see the point in strapping a sleeping baby into a car seat every day, just to drive her a short distance. Besides, they would have to get a new set of everything—from a bottle warmer to a crib.

Little did I know that Grace would bring me an enormous amount of joy, love, and a depth of pure connection. I didn't realise that she would help me begin to see life differently and teach me lessons that I clearly had not been ready for when I was raising my own daughter. In my twenties and a new mother, I was harried by the long list of to-dos and dos and don'ts. I struggled as I learned how to feed and care for my baby girl, Ruki, while wanting to do it well without having a nervous breakdown. She slept all day and cried through the night, keeping me awake and feeling pathetic and helpless.

Focused on getting things done, I was not completely present to the magic of a perfect being that was entrusted to my care. I worried about a lot of things back then.

Was I spoiling my baby by holding her for too long? Should I get her used to sleeping in noisy surroundings or make her bedroom a sound-proof haven? Why hadn't she grown any teeth when all the babies her age in our neighbourhood had already sprouted a couple?

Now, in my forties, I was wiser, calmer, and more willing to go with the flow. My time as Grace's nanny was clearly meant to be; it was a significant part of my soul signature. Having a front-row seat to the magic and mystery of an infant growing into a baby and, then, a toddler, taught me life lessons I couldn't have learned in any university. I also discovered that everything we need for our growth is right here, if only we pay attention.

My greatest teacher was a spitting, drooling, and pooping baby who represented the magic, miracle, and mystery of creation. I was watching a beautiful life unfold in front of me.

I was given the gift of Grace.

Chapter 1

I Know What I Need

A two-month-old baby knows what she/he needs. They don't have to conduct an opinion poll amongst their peers, nor do they care about the adults in their life. They don't stop to consider the feelings of adults about what they want and whether it is okay to want it.

Usually, the adults take cues from a baby—is she/he fussy? If yes, what kind of fussy? Does she/he need a nap, milk, or a fresh diaper? No wonder bookstore shelves all around the world are sagging under the weight of volumes devoted to decoding a baby's cries. Because all parents know that the I-am-hungry cry is different from the I-am-wet cry, which is nothing like the I-need-you-to-hold-me cry.

When Grace is pulling on a bottle, she seldom drinks more than she needs, and she instinctively trusts her little body's signals. At noon, she may drink a whole bottle of formula; at 3 p.m., she may drink half a bottle; and an hour later, she may need just a small amount, enough to soothe her to sleep. When she is done, she simply pushes the bottle away or lets the nipple rest on her lower lip, which tells me that she has no inclination to guzzle any more.

A question to consider: are we guilty of feeding our

body way beyond its needs? How often do we listen to what our body asks of us?

No matter what our body needs, we presume that food is the only solution. But it isn't always food that our body needs. Sometimes, we are dehydrated and need fluids; at times, our body craves a nutritious meal; some days, we need a rejuvenating massage; and some days, we need more sleep.

Do we pay attention to what we are eating and stop eating when we have had enough? Not always, right? I am guilty of eating mindlessly. Netflix has more of my attention than the apple slices that I pop in my mouth. We eat as we type, text, and talk. Sadly, mindless eating has become the soother of our generation.

Eating to a schedule is great for stable blood sugar levels, but it may be a good idea to pay equal attention to being satiated, and babies do that quite well. I know that if I have a morning of busy physical activity planned, a high-carb breakfast would give me a great head start. But if I have spent a day mostly hunched over my laptop, a light meal of salad greens suits me much better than a plate of rice and lentils.

Babies do not eat beyond what their bodies need because they are aware of everything they experience. They know when they are feeling hungry or full, sad or mad, grumpy or content; they don't know how to hide these feelings.

Emotional eating is something that adults become habituated to, as a way to not feel their feelings. We live in a culture that frowns upon emotional expression unless someone is cutting us off on the freeway, or while watching a sport where it is legitimate to behave like a bunch of chimps escaped from the zoo.

When we feel an intense emotion and the need to share, the people we look up to are not always available. And, when they are, they sometimes do not know how to empathise with our situation. In the absence of people who can see and hear us, it is sometimes easier to turn to a pint of ice cream as it is more comforting to 'eat' our feelings and self-soothe.

It is not uncommon for many of us to reach for a pill when we feel a monster headache grab hold of our temples. Sometimes, a headache is simply our body's plea for a time out. A nap, a walk in nature, deep breaths of fresh air, or an open conversation with a trusted friend will often cure it.

Worshipping the myth that 'we need to do more to have more and be more' makes us ignore our body's signals to slow down. I have heard folks declare with pride that they can easily function on four hours of sleep, almost as if it were a badge of honour. A fiercely competitive society and work culture has us strapped to the feeling that if we don't do as much as other successful people, we won't be enough.

Babies know better. When Grace is tired of playing with her vast assortment of toys, she digs her knuckles into her eyes and starts to fuss. That is her signal to me, which says: 'Hey! I am running out of steam here and need a nap. Help me!'

Grace naps anytime she needs to and according to her schedule. Some days, she takes two naps—midmorning and late afternoon; some days, she naps for five to six hours at a stretch; other days, she decides that forty winks will do just fine. But she always lets me know when she needs her forty winks. No toy can please her, and trying to hold her when she is grumpy is like trying to hold a bagful of monkeys.

After a nap, she wakes up smiling. Soon, she is cooing and gurgling and babbling, an angel of supreme happiness. Feeling her soft red hair on my chin as she snuggles in my arms, I ponder the lesson this holds for me.

Babies can nap anytime they like. You and I don't enjoy the luxury of an anytime nap, but we can choose to pay attention to our body's signals. For me, that sometimes means cutting the lights instead of curling up with my iPad or putting my novel away and turning in even though the plot has me on tenterhooks. It could even mean using weekend afternoons to catch up on sleep lost during a hectic travelling week or slowing down my pace on a day when I am feeling overwhelmed or saying no to the energy-zappers in my life—chronic complainers, sugary foods, and a mile-long to-do list.

Babies trust their needs. But, as they grow up, dos and don'ts begin to dominate their lives and their natural instinct disappears. As the years roll by, we begin to push back our needs while taking care of everyone else. In a life filled with others' needs and schedules, 'me-time' slips out of our vocabulary. We begin to deny our needs while taking care of everyone else. We invest our energies in being the perfect son, the perfect mother, the perfect friend, and the perfect wife. 'I' comes last on our own list.

Taught to 'be nice', we grow into people-pleasers and manage others' lives so that everyone who matters will be happy. Everyone except ourselves. We do this at the cost of our own personal happiness. Somewhere along the way, approval-seeking becomes more important than authenticity.

We say Yes when we mean No. We let friends control our lives because we can't imagine our lives without their approval. We volunteer in committees and clubs denying ourselves family time, and we pick up after a partner who can't tell the difference between the living room and the laundry basket.

The next time there is a decision to make, it may be worthwhile to pause before conducting a poll of your options on Facebook. It may be a good idea to stop and consider how the choices available to you will serve you. Always pick the one that serves your highest good; see how it sits in your gut. There is a reason why people ask, 'What does your gut say?' That is where our personal truth lives. So, don't go looking for your decisions in other people's gut.

I need to remind myself that only I know what I need, because nobody knows me better than I do.

Grace always lets me know exactly what she needs; all I have to do is listen.

Grow Self-Trust

1. Close your eyes and recall a problem you are struggling with.
2. Consider what part of the possible solution is within your control.
3. Now, step out of your headspace and slip into your heart space where your true wisdom lives.

4. Ask your heart what the next best step might be.
5. Listen deeply and receive whatever comes through—words, images, colours, or a person's face.
6. Don't question anything; just accept it and know that, as you walk through your day and week, more will be revealed.

Chapter 2

I Live in the Moment

As long as a few basic needs—a full belly and a clean, dry diaper—are met, what is right here right now is all that matters to a ten-week-old baby.

It is a lesson that comes to me in the form of a simple multicoloured rattle I hold up for Grace.

Grace's hazel eyes lock on the rattle, every cell of her being concentrated and wholly engaged with that toy. She stares at the spectrum of colours, completely mesmerised by the shifting palette. She is not thinking about the bottle of formula that is in the warmer, nor is she obsessing over why it took a good thirty seconds of distressed wailing for the thick-headed adults in her life to figure out that she wanted to be held. For the moment, that rattle is her entire cosmos— she and the rattle, the rattle and her.

Grace has no concept of the past or future to derail her. This is all there is, the present moment.

There will come a time in Grace's life when past and future will become real concepts that collide into her view of the present. Babies comes into the world as a lump of clay who are moulded by the adults in their lives. How they choose to anchor concepts of the past and future will, as they grow older, determine how strong they are in adapting to life's challenges. For instance, if the parents are always obsessing over how their lives could have been different if they had made the right decision, their child learns to do the same.

The simple joy of fully living in the moment is something we have squandered as adults. Yesterday's failed plans and tomorrow's agendas rush to crowd our present. The rich beauty of an autumn leaf doing a slow, elegant earthward tumble is lost to us because of the melodramatic thoughts cartwheeling inside our head. 'How dare she insult me!' or 'I hate my job' or 'I'll never lose all this weight' The incessant mental chatter goes on and on.

So often, I walk past the flowering plant in my den, oblivious to the freshly bloomed yellow hibiscus. I find myself staring out the window, but I'm not seeing leaves and trees. My mind is far away, mulling over some ancient grudge or pondering the unfairness of life's injustices.

I remember a time when my husband and I drove off on a trip, leaving our garage door wide open. Our kind-hearted neighbour went inside our home, locked the garage door, and let herself out the front door.

Our minds are always working overtime. *Have I fed the dog? Should I clean the bathroom? Will I get the promotion? Is there enough milk to last us the week?*

We find it hard to ground ourselves in the present because we believe that the next moment holds something better, and if we could just get to that next moment, we would be happier. Our reality, however, is the nasty boss, the whiny wife, and the feeling of never being enough for anybody. So, we have bought into this notion that 'feeling better' waits for us in the next moment, tantalisingly out of reach. Hence, we are in chase mode all the time.

People spend hundreds of thousands of dollars on weekend retreats and expensive online courses to learn the art of meditation. But little do they know that meditation is the simple art of sitting still. It doesn't have to be a mystical mountaintop experience that is only achieved through cross-legged contortions.

For some of us, just getting a break from our chattering mind is the delicious first taste of peace.

The Buddhists teach the practice of mindfulness meditation. They teach that if you are drinking tea, every part of your being must focus on the tea—its aroma, heat, and texture. It is about being awake to the richness of the complete experience of drinking tea.

In my cup of tea are the pages I haven't written, chores that need to be done, and a quick mental stocktaking of the refrigerator's contents to assess whether I need to make dinner or not. The hot and steamy aroma of the Assam tea, its bittersweet taste, and the warmth that slides down my throat, disappear in my fugue state.

When we bring mindfulness to every life experience, our lives become richer. Babies do this by pure instinct. The key is to anchor our awareness to the moment.

Peeling potatoes can be a meditative experience.

Folding laundry can be a meditative experience.

Washing a sinkful of dirty dishes can be a meditative experience.

It is so simple, yet so hard to do. As I turn out the lights and slip under the sheets, my mind is still tangoing with tomorrow's to-do list. Pending emails and petty worries perch in the nooks and crannies of my head when I know I should simply focus on my breathing and let sleep overtake me.

So many of us live, not in present-time, but what I call 'drama-time'. We are mentally replaying arguments and slights from the past or the injustices we have been forced to endure. I know it is easy for me to slip into this almost unconsciously. Four hours later, I am still trapped in the spiral of an argument that I had with my husband. I replay the scene over and over until my neural pathways feel worn out. I chew over the things I could have said and failed to say which would have given me more control in the silly feud. My mind expertly excavates past scenarios where I was wronged. I arm myself with more ammunition for the next round.

But at some point, I have to stop myself and let it go.

If we are not stuck in the rut of the past, we are racing toward a fearful tomorrow. *How am I going to pay the mortgage this month?* or *What if I'm laid off?* or *What will the medical report say when the doctor's office calls?*

Bill Keane once said: 'Yesterday is history, tomorrow is a mystery, today is a gift of God, which is why we call it the present.' How often we stroll past an array of gifts in the present moment—the blazing beauty of autumn foliage, the whisper of the breeze that curls into a verdant tree, the tinkling of wind chimes from a neighbour's yard. Instead, we meander inside the mazes in our heads, often lost in dilemmas that may never come to pass.

When I watch Grace surrender to her rattle, it is a lesson for me to be awake and alive. Funny thing is, this is how you and I lived when we were babies. And somewhere along the way, we got lost, choosing to follow plot instead of character. We chase after yesterdays and play catch-up with tomorrows, forgetting one simple truth: there is only one place from where we create our past and future—the present.

Sometimes, it takes a perfect little being to remind us. Grace curls her fingers around the rattle and shakes her chubby fist. She is now fully engaged in the sounds the rattle makes, smiling and turning the rattle one way and, then, the other.

Live in the moment, she seems to say. It is all there is.

Practice Presence

1. Take an orange in your hand and start to peel it.
2. Inhale its citrusy aroma. Feel the texture of its skin.
3. Pop a wedge into your mouth and feel the juice burst all over your tongue as your teeth sink into its soft flesh.
4. Listen to the sounds of orange disintegrating in your mouth.
5. Savour the orange . . . all of it—its sight, smell, taste, feel, and sound.
6. Slow down and experience the richness of every moment as you go through life today.

Chapter 3

I See Magic Everywhere

Three-month-old Grace is playing in her crib while I warm her formula. When I bring the bottle to her, I find her absorbed in the mobile that twirls above her crib. It is a magical circle of butterflies in green, blue, mauve, and lavender that circle hypnotically to the music.

No matter how long she lies in her crib, staring at the same four butterflies circling in the same predictable fashion, her delight is fresh each time. Or, it might be fair to say, she brings a fresh pair of eyes to it each time. Her hazel eyes follow the butterflies, and her open-mouthed marvel is enchanting. She is utterly engaged in the simple wonder of the moment.

As I observe her complete fascination, a simple yet powerful lesson opens for me: there is magic in every moment, if we choose to be open to it.

I distinctly remember my first spring in Chicago, days after my family and I moved to a suburban apartment. Everywhere I looked, I was greeted by virgin beauty—acres of lush green grass, majestic weeping willows, pastel skies, and carpets of flowers. For someone who was used to India's dusty, crowded streets, my backyard offered a view of paradise. Every time I watched the cars at an intersection, I was struck by the symphony of the choreography as I was used to Indian roads where traffic moved in a chaotic and disorderly fashion. My eyes were experiencing something utterly new.

It is so easy to become jaded to this picturesque setting; it takes a conscious effort to preserve the magic: the emerald lawn outside my kitchen window, the green-to-gold autumn landscape, and the crystalline magic that drapes itself around stark-limbed trees at wintertime. Ten years later, it takes more mindfulness to stay present to this gorgeous beauty, but I do practise gratitude for it.

Why do we become numb to magic? One of the key reasons I suspect is that we desire mastery over our environment. For instance, as we stroll past the bushes and flowers in a garden, there is a need to name, label, and categorise the flowers. Every flower turns into a thesis. What is its name? Where did it originate? When does it grow? What does it need for optimum care? When we know enough, we feel a sense of accomplishment. Extending the garden metaphor, everywhere we look in the garden, we are reminded of burdensome chores that block the magic: *I need to mow the lawn, plant flowers, water the garden, and remember to buy Miracle-Gro . . .*

To simply lean back and enjoy the marvels of nature requires a Saturday trip to the Botanical Gardens for many of us. And, sadly, these days we are more concerned about how those floral displays will look through the camera of our phones than seeing them with our eyes.

I stop when I catch myself labelling and sorting the flowers. I don't really need to know everything about the flower; I can simply *be* with the flower. I can tune into the magic of the veined petals, the powerful fragrance, and the vivid colours. I experience the flower—all of what I see and do not see—and, in that moment, I am letting go of the need to know.

The magic is in the mystery, and that is a profound truth that a baby knows. Every time Grace looks at those swirling butterflies, her mind doesn't attach to what makes them go around or how the mobile attaches to the crib. She simply opens her heart to the beauty.

As we grow older, our senses grow numb. Life's worries crowd out the simple joys that surround us, and the overstimulated mind is no longer open to mystery and magic. Over time, we bring a world-weary view to not just natural beauty but also to the opportunities and people in our lives. We bring a mundane grey layer of monotony to how we see those we are in intimate relationship with.

A new romantic relationship is tantalising as is a new venture that promises an adrenaline rush. But, as the rush wears off, we lose interest and find ourselves on the lookout for the next source which will provide the same high we experienced. It is the circle of life—the honeymoon phase, where the magic is well and alive, must be replaced by the middle phase of the married years. Does this mean the magic is missing, gone, or vanished into the ethers? I have come to realise that the magic is in the unknowing. If we looked at our partner and saw everything we have always seen, the magic is over.

Maybe, this is why infidelity is so pervasive. Husbands and wives don't cheat because their new partner is prettier or a stud; they cheat because the magic is reawakened in the newness of the affair. They feel seen and heard and experience the magic of their uniqueness in the other's gaze, words, curiosity, and touch.

If only I would look, really look into my man's heart with all of mine. What would I see? I would see the limitless generosity he brings to our marriage, his wry sense of humour, his natural goodness, and his passion for music. But so often, all we choose to see are the humdrum and the annoying: boxers on the bathroom floor or how he leaves the toothpaste cap off. If we consider the depths we haven't yet plumbed in the relationship, magic is simply waiting to emerge.

It is all too easy to let the magic slip into the realm of the mundane. I find myself preoccupied with the dishes in my sink when the mere act of raising my head brings my attention to the window which overlooks lush green grass, birds hopping about, and my neighbour's dog sniffing around with pure canine purpose. But this takes a conscious decision to ground myself in the here and now.

As you stroll through nature, consciously take deep lungfuls of air. Make time to watch a cloud drift lazily across an expanse of sky. Close your eyes and inhale the warm steam of freshly brewed coffee. Listen to the soft whisper of a snowfall.

We have been given five senses. We are meant to use them and appreciate them. We are meant to feel the richness of life as it presents itself in every moment.

Grace opens and closes her fist, mesmerized by what her fingers can do as they curl and uncurl. She teaches me well.

Wake up to Magic

1. Watch a leaf, bird, flower, the sky, or your child.
2. Watch without attempting to label or understand. Be open to the nature of its beauty.
3. When you watch it the next time, see it with fresh eyes.
4. Reflect on your experience.

Chapter 4

I HAVE NEEDS, NOT PREFERENCES

When three-month-old Grace needs her diaper changed, she doesn't care who is doing the job as long as someone gets it done. All that matters to her is a fresh, dry, and feel-good Huggies. If she is fussy and needs to nap, it doesn't matter who rocks her to sleep as long as someone does. She doesn't care whether she is dressed in a pink onesie or a green one, she just needs to stay warm. This is because she lives in the space of complete trust and oneness, with no ability to differentiate.

It is when the 'self' starts to announce itself—usually around eighteen to twenty-four months of age—that the concept of separation and, therefore, preference begins to take root. This is the age when toddlers start to spit out their veggies and insist on a cookie, or experience separation anxiety at day care as they release their palms from Mommy's.

As children grow through teenage years, separation from authority figures increases. It is a necessary process as they begin to figure out who they are, what their opinions are, and how they create their niche in the world. A sense of self is imperative to establish one's identity at school, workplace, within social circles, and the world at large. After all, exercising preferences is part of the process. Biology over English, software engineer over energy auditor, and sci-fi over horror.

Those who grew up with strict disciplinarian parents sometimes find it challenging to exercise preferences. As adults, they have trouble making decisions, and often prefer to be led. All of us know adults who are simply unable to choose because the very notion of having a choice is an alien concept to them. Women who have been raised to believe that they are subservient to men, find it both fascinating and frightening that there is a world out there where other women exercise choices every single moment of their lives.

My own mother is a case in point. Born and raised in India by a domineering mother (and a father who left such matters to his wife), she had little say in significant life choices. Getting a college education was a significant milestone. With a bachelor's degree in science and math, my mother was very keen to further her education and get a master's degree. However, my grandparents—her mother, in particular—had other ideas. My mother was reminded that a woman's place was in the home, that she ought to concern herself with matters of housekeeping and domestic efficiency so she could make some man a dutiful wife. Having lost the power to choose at an early age, she simply bowed down and accepted her fate. From that day onwards, my mother rarely made decisions. After her marriage, she depended on my father to make decisions, and when he was unavailable, we, as her children, stepped in and did the needful. She was sixty-eight when she died, but, for all of those sixty-eight years, she continued to consult with her mother before making the simplest of decisions like how much to pay the temple priest, where to shop for the best saris, and what day might be an auspicious day to make an investment. In a world where we are constantly forced to make decisions for ourselves or for those who matter to us, it is a daily struggle for an adult who is unable to articulate and/or stand up for what they need.

On the other hand, when we are so defined by our separate self, we risk disconnection. The separation solidifies to an extent where we lose our connection to a larger whole, and the parts become more important than the whole. We socialise with people who go to the kinds of plays and movies that we do; we join Meetup groups where we can belong to a tribe of like-minded folks. Eventually, we begin to identify completely with the commonalities we share.

We don't always tune into the truth that we all came from the same place and will return there someday. And the time we share here is one of common struggles, joys, and pains for all of us. If we lived with that perspective, ours would be a world where co-operation would trump competition because we would all feel supported by one another.

Instead, we sort people into categories and sub-categories: Asian, American-Indian, Punjabi, Malayali, Muslim, bisexual, etc. We align our preferences with those who are more like us and distance ourselves from those who seem unfamiliar and, in extreme cases, threatening. Separation has an ugly downside to it. We alienate people who live in certain neighbourhoods, eat foods we have never heard of, listen to music we have zero familiarity with, vote for a particular party, or pray to a God of their choice in a unique house of worship.

Preferences aren't entirely bad—if we just contained them to Thai food over Mediterranean, chick lit over memoir, and rollerblading over NBA. Life would be great if our differences in tastes were as simple as Butter Pecan over Double Chocolate Chip or *General Hospital* over *Keeping Up with the Kardashians*.

It is when we attach morality to non-moral choices that matters get really out of hand. For instance, we have a tendency to assume that someone who watches a lot of reality television is probably not as intelligent as someone who tunes into PBS. If you listen to rap, you are hanging out with the wrong crowd. If you have tattoos on your skin, you are likely to be violent and dangerous.

Watching my mother's utter subservience while I was growing up, I vowed never to be like her. My conviction— if you are a doormat, people will stomp all over you. I admired strong women who had opinions and expressed themselves with confidence and poise. I wanted to belong to that world. But, in my desire to move as far away as I could from her set point, I overcompensated and became a radical. I became attached to my world view because I believed that it defined me, and this made me insufferably stubborn. I vowed that I would never settle for an arranged marriage and was persistent about the idea of finding wedded bliss on my terms. This was the source of several heated exchanges between me and my parents as things had to go *my* way. I wasn't open to other points of view or modes of navigating life.

It has taken a lot of self-awareness to crumble some of those long-standing walls and learn to move through life with grace. As long as I was attached to my preferences of how something should unfold or how someone must behave, I was blind to the powerful concept of letting go. Today, my attitude is much more fluid and life flows more smoothly. When I am inspired to teach a workshop on a subject that I am interested in, I consciously let go of how it will all develop—where I will teach it, how many students will enrol, and how much money I will make. I do have a preference on all these aspects, but I try not to attach to them. I simply recognise that my job is to show up for the assignment, step into it with power and poise, and surrender the rest to the Universe. I trust that the Universe will navigate the parts that I cannot control. This serves me well. It opens me to numerous possibilities and the result is exactly what it needs to be. Miraculously, things go much better than I imagine when I get out of my own way.

With no preferences, Grace is pure openness. She doesn't know how to hate or judge or exclude. You and I, too, came into the world with this knowing. We lived in that blissful state until we were about two years old, and then we let our 'self' take over.

Why is it so hard for us to honour another human being as the product of their upbringing and circumstance? Why are some folks better and that, too, for the flimsiest reasons: because they live in the right neighbourhood or possess a certain skin colour? What is wrong if some people pray five times a day and others question the very existence of God? Why do we judge an entire community as dangerous, untrustworthy, or uncouth? This is the basis of differentiation and division, the beginning of war between peoples and nations.

Grace has no clue that my skin is several shades darker than her lily-white complexion. She treats me with the same love as she treats all her significant relationships.

She doesn't understand differences yet. There will, undoubtedly, come a time when she does, and, then, she will have lost a precious piece of her innocence, a prerequisite to her earthly journey.

But, for now, all I need to do is offer her a warm bottle, hold her, keep her safe, and soothe her. It could be Mommy, it could be Daddy, or it could be me. She is contented as long as her needs are taken care of.

How I wish my own life was as uncomplicated as Grace's. With her inspired guidance, I can certainly remind myself that it is easier to flow with the current than trying to swim against it. Life works harmoniously, and I am grateful for a baby's wisdom that reconnects me to a truth I, too, brought into this world with me and have strayed away from.

Go with the Flow

1. Think of a problem and your attachment to how it must resolve.
2. Ask yourself what might happen if you opened your heart to a different outcome from the one you are attached to.
3. Tune into where your resistance comes from and why.
4. Consciously open yourself to the idea of flowing with life and breathe easy.

Chapter 5

I Can't Crawl before I do Tummy Time

Every baby is programmed for milestones. But every baby is also completely content to progress at her/his own pace. Guided by instinct and the infinite intelligence of the Universe, a baby simply obeys natural law.

Grace took her own sweet time with her early milestones.

In keeping with the paediatrician's advice, her parents and I lay her down on her tummy for a specific length of time two to three times every day. We were told that this would encourage her to raise her head and strengthen her neck muscles over time.

Grace was perfectly happy to lie on her back for about three-and-a-half months; she was in no hurry to change things. Enforced tummy time elicited loud protests. Clearly unconcerned with her paediatrician's timeline, she was following her internal prompts.

Then came the time when lying on her back wasn't enough. She was ready for the next level of adventure of growing up. As soon as I lay her down on the floor mat, she flipped over. Now, she was enjoying the top-down view of her world—even if she wasn't at an exciting elevation yet. She was still working on lifting her head up.

Doing tummy time with her was a brand-new concept for me. When I was raising my daughter in India, her paediatrician never brought it up. Babies just flipped over when they were ready to, and parents weren't expected to intervene and accelerate results. My two-month-old daughter would push herself to one side and work on her muscles, pushing past the hump of her arm. Early on, she would fall many times, frustrated but also exhausted. Not willing to give up, she would try again. Once she had mastered it to an extent, she worked diligently until she perfected it. It was endearing to watch.

A lot of rewiring happens in a baby's brain when they go from lying on their back and staring at the ceiling to lying on their tummy and staring at a patch of floor. When we tried to push Grace to do tummy time, it probably didn't feel natural. Maybe, she wasn't ready, and maybe, we were pushing her towards a milestone that was still some time away.

A baby never reaches for a milestone that she/he is not ready for. It is an internal rhythm they tune into. It was the same with Grace. Something inside her urged her to get on with the next step in her evolution when the time was right. And she was perfectly content to get to it when it felt right.

It is hard to imagine a five-month-old, in any part of the world, being depressed because they just didn't hit the tummy-turn milestone soon enough. Babies would never call themselves 'idiots' or 'morons' or 'slow' simply because they didn't reach a milestone at a certain time—even if some well-respected academic professor published findings that indicated they were developmentally behind. Babies just do their own thing, and they are all on target, in their own time.

As we grow into adulthood, we forget the truth about natural law and buy into societal law. We become impatient and attached to our timelines with respect to careers, relationships, and the assets we wish to own. Success has become a mass-produced assembly line construct. It has come to be defined by titles, salaries, possessions, club memberships, and access to privileges—coveted milestones on the path to success.

Browse online and you find a zillion 'get-rich-quick' schemes. There are eager buyers who hanker after e-Courses that teach them how to drop a staggering number of pounds by swallowing pills, start earning a six-figure income in thirty days, or find their soul mate in five simple steps.

Musicians rehearse and perfect their performance for years before they even get on stage to perform in front of large audiences. Many of them start with local gigs; they take whatever work comes their way and hone their skills as they step, rung by rung, on the ladder to somewhere. On the other hand, writers entertain this fantasy that the first book they write must be grabbed by a famous publishing house for an impressive advance and, then, go on to sell a million copies and make it to the New York Times Bestseller list. Sometimes, it takes writing a book or two to perfect the craft before one is ready to pen a publish-worthy one.

Looking back on my life, I can definitely say that I am guilty of this fantasy. I recall the days I slaved over a piece of prose, got frustrated, and mentally quit. Desperate, I tried to imitate my favourite writers: Elizabeth Berg, Chitra Banerjee Divakaruni, and Anita Shreve. I suffered self-doubt and declared that I would never make it as a writer. And, of course, I wanted a publishing contract from a reputed house (a fat advance would be very nice, thank you) long before I was halfway done with my manuscript. Gullible to the fantasy, I fell victim to a pay-to-publish scheme, hoodwinked by a publishing house that had its head offices in London (or so they said). 'Pay us a certain amount of money and we will publish your manuscript and launch it with panache,' was their promise. When the firm set up offices in India, my fantasy went on overdrive. My dear husband sold our brand-new family car to finance my dream, a dream that ended in a handful of charred ashes. The publisher reneged on every promise made and I, the naïve writer, had failed to do a background check to ascertain their credentials. It was a costly mistake, one that taught me a few valuable lessons: Wait. Be patient. Timing is everything.

The journey of writing and rewriting, being rejected by twenty-five agents, and being turned down by various magazine editors made me grow, both as a writer and a person . . . not the publishing contract I eventually got. The pleasure of arranging sentences on a page is a high. When done mindfully, writing is its own reward as it is stressful to write with the expectation that there is some grand prize waiting at the end of it. Practice is everything in the pursuit of perfection.

I wish, at that time, I had had Grace then to remind me that I was exactly where I needed to be. Time, practice, and life experience were necessary next steps in my evolution as a writer. I had to prepare the field and nourish the soil. I had to scatter the seeds and wait for sunshine and rain to do their job; I had to get the bad first drafts written. Only then could the polished work begin to emerge. Readiness is all about cultivating the conditions and being respectful of the timing.

Trust is such an important aspect of that journey. I guess that is why Martin Luther King Jr's quote continues to speak to me decades later: 'Faith is taking the first step even when you can't see the whole staircase.' It is hard for a lot of us to do that. We like being in control and taking charge. Surrender and release are wonderful spiritual concepts in a book, but tough to practice when life requires us to.

The title of the book, *What's in the Way Is the Way: A Practical Guide for Waking Up to Life* by Mary O'Malley, speaks volumes to me. What we judge as obstacles in our path are there to help us grow—whether it is learning to love oneself before finding a loving partner, taking responsibility for one's actions before attracting healthy relationships, or letting go of the need to blame to develop an attitude of self-reflection. This is exactly what was in Grace's way. Her uncoordinated fingers unable to curl around and hold a rattle, undeveloped muscles that couldn't help her to crawl, and teeter-totter balance before she learned to walk. But they *were* the way. She had to master hand-eye coordination (to hold), moving one knee followed by the next (to move forward), and gain a sense of balance (to stand) before she could walk without plopping down on her butt.

Waiting is powerful. While we wait, we prepare, and what we desire, eventually, finds us. We are then ready to receive it and use it well. But this is so incompatible with the instant gratification culture we live in. We want something, and we want it *now*—and we can have it *now*. Whether it is the desire to know how the Fibonacci sequence of numbers works, where 855 Lincoln Park is, or where to find a real Tibetan bowl, we have the answers at our fingertips. Our lives are Googled.

I think back to my childhood. My parents had to put away a certain sum of money every single month to buy anything they needed—whether it was a refrigerator, blender, or television set. When that refrigerator eventually came home, our joy was unbounded. We had worked hard for it, and we now owned it. That special sense of accomplishment and satisfaction made the waiting a period of rich anticipation and the receiving of it so much sweeter. To this day, I remember the thrilling sensation of cold air kissing my face when I opened the refrigerator door and peeked in with utter reverence.

A perfect example of the rewards that come with waiting is Diana Nyad, the champion swimmer who created a world record at the age of sixty-four when she swam from Cuba to Florida—a distance of 177 kilometres that she covered in fifty-three straight hours—after four failed attempts. She achieved her dream when *she* was ready, not on her timeline and not by taking any shortcuts.

For now, Grace is enjoying her brand-new world view from her tummy. It may be a limited view, but she is perfectly content, judging by her gleeful gurgles. Every time she manages to roll onto her tummy, she flashes me a smile of triumph. This is exactly where she is meant to be, and she celebrates that milestone.

Grace is a good teacher. I am so grateful because she reminds me to honour every milestone on my road.

Be Where You Are

1. Look at where you are in life right now and identify a source of discontent. It could be anything—from relationships to career and money.
2. Ask yourself what is good about where you are. It could be that the money you have is adequate for your needs. Or the romantic relationship you don't have is your time to get clear about who you wish to attract.
3. Close your eyes and experience a moment of gratitude for where you are.
4. Know in the deepest part of your being that the next door will open when you are ready to walk through it.

Chapter 6

I FEEL YOUR ENERGY

Like most babies, Grace feels the energy people bring into her space. She has no words to communicate her feelings. She is, however, intimately connected to how her body feels when someone holds her or talks to her way before language bubbles up to her conscious experience. Her response to people is a direct consequence of what she feels in her body.

If I brought in frazzled or distracted energy into Grace's space, she sensed it immediately. Consequently, she would fuss more, and I would have a harder time getting her to calm down. As I grew more aware of this truth, I engaged in a daily practice before I entered her space. I would pull up to the Bibby residence, park the car, close my eyes, and take a few deep breaths to 'centre and enter' her world. It was a way of punctuating my entry into her life by tuning out the distractions and dilemmas of my worldly concerns. I would say a prayer that went something like this: 'May I bring safe, loving, and calm energy into her space.'

Babies have no ability to judge, label, or sort. But they seem to come equipped with energy sensors. Not yet ready to make choices based on logic or reason, they definitely feel our energy—happy, anxious, distracted, or disengaged.

Adult motivations are definitely more mind-based. We develop judgments as we engage with life, people, and circumstances. Adults who are cheated out of something that was rightfully theirs may tend to be suspicious and have trouble trusting others. They build emotional walls so that they can protect themselves from getting hurt again. Over time, they may come to believe that this is the safest way to be, especially, when there is a pay-off. Someone who has been abandoned or stepped over as a child may expect to be abandoned in her/his adult relationships. A person who equates being in control with strength, does everything she/he can to stay strong and abhors any sign of weakness in others.

We have all heard some version of these statements: 'I don't like the look of that guy', 'She doesn't feel very safe', or 'Something about him weirds me out.' But, often, we are not sure what is going on. As we grow into adulthood, we disengage more and more from how we feel in our bodies. Trained to be logical, we take up residence in our heads, often ignoring signals from our bodies: 'Don't trust that guy', 'Say no to her', or 'Don't make that left turn.' We override the subtle hints. As we get hit by the proverbial two-by-four real-life situation, we begin to learn our lessons. Often, this is the sad truth behind the purple bruises and broken ribs of women who ignore the red flags from an abusive or controlling partner. They dismiss the playful pushing and shoving as non-threatening even when something about it doesn't feel right. When their partner insists on isolating them from close friends and family, they explain it away as: 'He loves me so much, he wants me all to himself.'

Experts in the area of domestic abuse say that the most common refrain they hear from women who suffer extreme forms of verbal abuse is: 'He never hit me.' These women ignore the negative energy their men emanate and swat away concerns with: 'I must be imagining it' or 'I'm making too much of this.'

I can recall instances when my body alerted me about someone I was meeting for the first time—a tightness in my gut, a recoiling, a feeling of inexplicable threat. And this happened when the person in question had not even uttered a single word. I didn't know it at the time, but their energy was speaking to my energy. The shifty look in their eyes or an aggressive posture were physical manifestations of that energy and betrayed their unspoken intent. Before I learned to trust my intuition, I tried to ignore those messages from my body and passed them off as me being paranoid for no reason. Over time, I have come to trust these signals because all the ignored signals from my past have come back to bite me. I know now that my body seldom lies.

Working in a hospice facility, I used to come home on certain days laden with energies that didn't feel like me. I usually don't feel anxious or tight in my body, but after a volunteering stint in hospice, it was not uncommon for me to lie awake in bed with a racing heart while I wondered why I was feeling that way. A teacher pointed out that the patient I was visiting may have been in a great deal of fear about dying or their family members were gripped by the fear of losing them, and I was absorbing that energy. Being an empath, I can cry over an exquisite sunset just as easily as I can feel someone else's strong emotions in my body. Since then, I have learned to protect my energy before I enter the room of someone who is at death's door. I pray to Archangel Michael, the angel of safety and protection, or I visualise a ball of golden light—the light of God—surrounding me. These practices have helped me safeguard my energy boundaries. It enables me to give all of myself emotionally to the other without absorbing any fear and anxiety.

Babies are like super-absorbent diapers. I have heard of babies who wouldn't stop crying when a certain adult picked them up. It is likely that the adult in question was high-strung or of a nervous disposition, and the baby just felt the negative energy.

Given that babies have not developed their logical left brain, they rely entirely on instinct. Dr Jill Bolte Taylor illustrates this energy theory in her memoir, *My Stroke of Insight: A Brain Scientist's Personal Journey,* that chronicles her stroke and miraculous recovery. As she lost her functional brain—language, order, and cognition—she found herself completely functioning in egoless, right-brain mode. Physically, she was thirty-something, but cognitively she entered the pure, innocent, and childlike state where she felt people's energy and could immediately sense whether they were safe or not. She was only able to relax with those who 'engaged' with her—people who looked right at her when they spoke and touched her with gentle care. If a nurse or doctor bustled around the room taking her vitals and addressed her without making eye contact, she received a vibe that felt disconnected.

Babies are the same. They know—from the way they are being held and the way adults respond to their needs for a fresh diaper or a calming cuddle—whether your energy feels secure, distracted, or unsafe.

Unfortunately, I wasn't as aware of this when I was a new mother. With Time as my master, I focused on checking things off a list. Bath time, nap time, bed time, snack time—it was all sacrosanct. Looking back, I wish I had tuned into what my daughter's energy needs were and responded in kind. Maybe, there were days when she needed a longer cuddle or a shorter nap. Maybe, my neighbour's energy didn't feel good to her, and I may have politely thrust her into their arms. I think about how silly marital squabbles stopped me from fully engaging with my baby girl because there was a veritable tsunami going on inside my head about how wrong my husband was and how right I was.

Now that I am older and wiser, my experience helps me engage with a baby differently. You don't have to be family to practice this; you just have to be mindful. Anytime you are about to enter a baby's space—or anyone's space for that matter—an energy check is a good idea. If you have just had an argument with your spouse or got off the phone after a haranguing conversation with a service provider who pushed your buttons, stop and slow down for a few moments. Breathe deeply and consciously, filling up and emptying out. Centre yourself before you engage with the baby.

If you are stressed and you pick up a fussy baby who needs you to help them calm down, it is hard to pull calming energy from within you. Instead, their irritable crying will frustrate you further and the negative energy in the situation will multiply.

Do yourself and your baby a favour—be responsible for the energy you bring into their space. The cable guy you were arguing with about your exorbitant monthly bill will soon recede into the past as an aspect of a difficult day. But the relationship you are nurturing with your baby is forever.

When my energy field is calm, Grace calms down easily with me. I am relaxed in the way I hold her, rock her, and contain her. And, within moments, she is able to relax and drift into the land of dreams.

Body Scan Meditation

1. Close your eyes and take a deep centring breath, a breath that brings all of you into the present moment.
2. Scan each part of your body and see where you feel a tight knot of energy.
3. As you breathe into it, visualise a stream of pure white light dissolve the knot.
4. Keep breathing in and out until your energy has softened.

Chapter 7

I like Being Treated
with Tenderness

When Grace whines and grinds her face into my shoulder, she is sending me a clear signal—she is tired and either needs a bottle or a nap. Probably, both. A bottle that will lead her gently to a nap is my best bet. Even as she is wriggling and squirming in my arms, I know one thing for sure—she is asking to be treated with tenderness. This is when a rhythmic backrub or soothing shush—as I offer the words: 'Calm down, sweetie'—helps her settle down. If I allow her distress to perturb me or rush around, trying to find a fix, she becomes more agitated. I need to stay grounded and just be the space to contain her tetchy behaviour.

We do pretty well in applying this technique with babies, but we lose track of it while dealing with adults. It is so easy to forget that an annoyed or angry adult is acting out, fussing about something that is not going right in their life. It could be the guy fuming behind us in the Starbucks line or our boss who can't stop yelling and blaming everyone else for the department's issues. Such behaviour feels as if it is being directed at us, and we take it personally.

I, too, have felt attacked and retorted in self-defence many times. I have certainly felt abused by friends who projected their unmet needs or frustrations on me. Turning the other cheek, as Gandhi suggests, does not come easily at such a time. I am no noble emotional container. I have cut off friendships because of something a friend said or did which I know I need not have taken personally. My self-indulgent behaviour has often caused me to see the other as the offender instead of looking inwards.

Granted, adult interactions are way more complicated than ministering to the needs of a fussy baby. Mind games, ego projections, and personality differences stir the pot. The truth is that a full-grown adult sometimes has more trouble articulating their needs than a baby. We expect others to know how to deal with us and work things out. But how many of us were well-schooled in conflict resolution? On a side note, if we were absolutely honest, many parents will concede that even a whining baby can trigger deep, unexpressed emotions in us. But because Grace is unable to verbalise what is going on inside her, she has our sympathy. We do not extend the same sympathy to an adult who has the ability to verbalise. Or, do they? What we don't realise is that many of us don't have the language for emotional expression. We don't know how to convey that we are hurt or sad or grieving or angry. There are layers of judgments wrapped around feelings and expressions.

If we can remain calm enough and not be triggered by others' issues, we soon realise that people who act out are simply unleashing their internal demons. It is more about them and less about us. There is wisdom in the saying: 'Hurt people hurt people.'

Irish theologian and teacher, John O'Donohue, says: 'We can never see another's experience; we only see their behaviour.' That is not to say we should simply let everyone trample over us with hobnailed boots. Healthy boundaries are important. When we respect ourselves, we let others know they should do the same. It is a way of saying: 'I love and respect myself. I won't tolerate being treated badly.'

Most of the times, if we choose not to respond to others' bad behaviour, they will leave us alone. An adult's resentment or irritation is usually a socially acceptable cry for help. When a baby cries out of fear or even discomfort, we rush towards them, embrace them, and drive the boogeyman away. When faced with a hurting adult, we forget the value of tenderness. We are more apt to think resentful thoughts which, eventually, turn into violent ones.

The word 'violence' usually conjures up images of gangs, guns, and war. But a teacher once pointed out that violence begins in the mind. And, if everything begins with a thought, many of us are guilty of thinking violent thoughts during the course of our day.

Violent thoughts can be self-directed, such as *I'm not worth it, I'll never have love in my life,* or *I never do anything right.* When our head is crowded with such thoughts, we feel the need to defend and protect when someone injures us. Or, we perceive something they said as a threat. When that threat takes the form of thinly veiled sarcasm, being ignored, or spoken to in an unkind tone, we retaliate in kind. Tenderness is the last thing on our minds.

No matter where we come from, who we are, and what we do, all of us simply want to be treated with tenderness.

Examine your own life and relationships, and you will find that, for the most part, you navigate towards those who treat you with kindness and steer clear of those who don't—except when it is the family that shares your genes and the family you go home to every night. This is exactly why our deepest conflicts and angst erupt in our most intimate relationships. All boundaries vanish in the moment of our heated conversations.

The next time your spouse or child snaps at you, pause. Bite your tongue. Hold the retort back. Say in the kindest tone you can muster, 'Honey, where is that irritation coming from?' This will feel awkward if you are not used to having such conversations. But if you persevere, you will find that, over time, you will help them own their behaviour and not simply make it about you.

When you treat people with tenderness, you give them a gift. Wherever there is a wound, tenderness is the best balm. Its restorative powers are life-changing.

When you are feeling emotionally overwrought, wouldn't you like a touch of tenderness, too?

Grace's loose limbs tell me that she trusts enough to let go and relax into being soothed. When I hold her in a circle of energy that attempts to diffuse the tension instead of adding to it, she is able to let go. Trust a baby to help you remember the basics.

Reflection

1. Reflect on the words by Jane Austen: 'There is no charm equal to tenderness of heart.'

2. Journal your thoughts. Think about what tenderness of the heart means to you. Does tenderness bring more strength into a situation? Does it transform the energy from destruction into something resembling redemption?

Chapter 8

I Don't Enjoy Overstimulation

Six-month-old Grace was fussing a great deal one afternoon. When I offered her a bottle, she pushed it away. I bounced her on my knees, hoping that would soothe her. I rocked her, sang to her, and rubbed her back, moving my palm in comforting concentric circles. Nothing worked. She just wasn't happy, and, soon, I was out of ideas.

Racking my brain for something that would help her, I lay her down on the floor mat. Then, I picked up a multicoloured rattle and shook it loudly. When that didn't work, I picked up one of her favourite furries that made a funny sound when squeezed. Next, I held up a wind-up toy that danced and bounced and clanked.

Grace would have none of it and continued to fuss.

All of a sudden, it hit me. I dropped everything, scooped her up, locked eyes with her, and started to talk to her in a calm, soothing voice. Sure enough, she quieted down within seconds, and her eyelids started to droop.

Grace was communicating a specific discomfort, and I was actively drowning out her message with all manner of distractions. I was overstimulating her. Naïvely, I believed that if I rattled colourful objects in her face and made enough noise to get her attention, she would stop fussing.

But she didn't need more stimulation. Babies are in touch with their discomfort, and they can stay in that zone, feeling the unpleasant feelings—until acknowledged and attended to. They are not seeking to be distracted from the source of their discomfort. That was a valuable lesson.

As adults, we have learned the art of distracting ourselves from what doesn't feel good, whether it frightens, intimidates, overwhelms, irritates, or threatens us. A friend of mine has to have the TV on all the time, even if he is not paying any attention to what is on it; he cannot stand the sound of silence. Some people need the radio when they are driving, whether it is tuned to the sports channel, music, or the news. My husband and I have different views on this. I simply want to be surrounded by silence in the car, whereas he enjoys audio input whilst driving.

Maybe, we have become so used to living in a noisy world that silence has become awkward and uncomfortable. We have squandered the art of simply 'staying with' and 'feeling' our way through an experience that doesn't feel good.

Often, a difficult task in front of us makes us procrastinate and scramble towards some form of stimulation. When I am trawling through Facebook, reading and commenting on posts instead of writing, I know that I am in distraction mode. I really ought to park my butt in a chair and put pen to paper. But the fear that stalks every writer when they face a blank page—the fear of having nothing worthwhile to say—

keeps me stalling. I check my email, read articles that don't matter a whit, or click on a link that soon leads me to another and, before I know it, I am down the rabbit hole of the Internet, completely distracted from what I ought to be doing. Forty-five minutes later, I decide it is too late to start writing because it is time to head out to an appointment. I fill my day with enough errands and chores that take me away from the one thing I should be doing, the one thing that gives me the greatest pleasure when I get right down to it—writing.

How do I overcome my distractions and stop procrastinating? The first step is to stop judging my output. I have made peace with the truth that what shows up on the page doesn't always sparkle, nor will I always be rewarded with a gush of words the moment I turn on the writing faucet. Some days, it is a dribble, some days it is a steady but finite flow, and on others, I cannot keep up with the inspiration that pours onto the page. But here is what I need to remember: it is all good.

Some people who are grieving find it comforting to hide in overstimulation, for it lets them remain in the fog of a neutral reality. The most common response I hear when I ask a grieving client how she is coping is: 'I'm staying really busy.' Distractions can be wonderful when unpleasant feelings overwhelm us. We don't have to face the root of our discomfort, especially, when something difficult needs to be addressed.

Overstimulation triggers anxiety in some of us. I am awful at multitasking. Talking on the cell phone when I am trying to help myself to lunch and trying to find my keys all at once is enough to make me feel crazy. Believe it or not, I cannot even eat lunch and read at the same time. Until I knew better, I judged myself for not being able to do what most of America does expertly (or so it seems). It made me feel slow, inefficient, and somewhat old.

What rescued me from my own belief was a personality test I took. According to the test, my natural style is slow and single-focused. I do my best work when I focus on one thing with no distractions. That test freed me from feeling that I wasn't enough. Today, I also know that time and space are finite concepts in our earthly experience. If I don't get everything done today, I am not rattled by it. Tomorrow is another day, and if I die before I get there, well, I did the best I could with what I had. I don't beat myself up any more about productivity, goals, and suchlike.

Neale Donald Walsch, author of the bestselling *Conversations with God* series, says, 'Perfection is the obstacle of creation and the enemy of achievement. At some point it may serve you to decide that a particular project or undertaking is complete. Seeking excellence is one thing; never finding anything totally satisfactory is another.' I say, amen to that! This simple piece of wisdom has turned my life around. I get a lot done because I have stopped pursuing perfection and stimulating myself with all kinds of distractions for fear of never achieving it.

Our world makes a dazzling variety of distractions available all the time. Malls that tempt you with their neon displays and discount sales, nightclubs and pubs with strobe lights and ear-splitting music, and constant unstoppable entertainment and information via the Internet are enough to make us dizzy.

Attached to cell phones and electronic gizmos, we have become programmed to remain in a state of high alert. Consider what happens when your cell phone dings a message or a Facebook message pops up on your screen. We are primed to respond. Somehow, we have forgotten that things can wait while we take a moment to pause, breathe, or relax. Even when we drink coffee with a friend, words fill the air. A moment of silence is very uncomfortable. It is as though we need to keep talking and doing and feeding our senses all the time.

Used to a constant level of overstimulation, people who are under-stimulated also become triggered by anxiety. Boredom is a potential anxiety trigger. Standing in line at the grocery store, being stuck in traffic, and having to wait at the doctor's office can be uncomfortable for a lot of people. Having to stop means having to focus on thoughts, feelings, or bodily sensations that we don't want to feel. Surrounding ourselves with noise—ours or others'—helps us ignore the pain in our lives.

Anne LeClaire writes in her memoir, 'Noise is a form of violence done to us, but we have become so accustomed to it that it barely registers, like a car alarm that blares on and on but which no one heeds. Sound systems have become part of our communal landscape, inescapable in supermarkets, shopping malls, ballparks, elevators, coffee shops and restaurants, office waiting rooms and hospitals. It's as if we have come to believe that silence is a void that must be filled whatever the cost. We no longer know how to be still. We no longer know how to be alone. We seem to require constant and relentless input. We are addicted to sensory overstimulation.'[1]

How do you invite overstimulation into your life? What are the distractions that keep you from what you need to attend to? What stops you from fully engaging with what you know you should?

For some, it may be that dreaded phone call to a grieving co-worker—because they fear they don't have the right words. For others, it may be the laziness about getting to the gym and getting on a treadmill, making that doctor's appointment to address a suspicious symptom, writing that email for a job interview, apologising to a friend for the hurtful comment spoken in a moment of rage, or not being able to decline an invitation for fear of offending a family member.

To stay away from what we know we should focus on, we eat, drink, text, waste time online, play video games, work twelve-hour days, and cram our to-do lists with enough tasks to kill us. In effect, we are running scared. We are running away from the thing or person or next step we don't want to face.

The grandest illusion of all is the belief that the more we do, the more value we have. We tell ourselves that all this overstimulation has a purpose. When we hit the bed at night, our worthiness is about having checked off those twenty-six jobs on our list. We feel validated. We feel efficient. We feel good. We also feel empty, because in the deepest part of ourselves, we know this doesn't make the cut. So, we wake up the next morning and try to do more, be more, have more. Life becomes a race without a finish line.

Then, there is dutiful busyness and pointless busyness. We do have to get stuff done at work, home, and for our loved ones. But then some of us also engage in virtuous busyness. Cleaning the church, volunteering at the food bank, or driving seniors to their appointments can be a wonderful and selfless form of service but not if we are using those tasks to keep ourselves from facing what needs to be faced.

Culture and society provide us more and more avenues of overstimulation than ever before. Through all the handheld devices we own, we invite politicians, sports figures, and reality TV stars into our bedrooms, all in an effort to turn away from our emotional baggage.

A baby comes into the world completely free, without any baggage. After nine months in the quiet and relative predictability of the utero-home, a baby enters our world and has to deal with bright lights, machines that whir and grind, and the rambunctiousness of an older sibling. No wonder they get fussy. But the baby's instinctive intelligence tells them that it is time to shut down when things in their physical world get overwhelming. And sometimes, they need an adult's help in getting quiet.

A meditative state is unique to each one of us. For me, the act of sitting cross-legged, my favourite prayer shawl draped around me, and tuning into my inner guidance gets me into that space. Some like a walk in the woods where the quiet whisper of the wind calms them. Gazing at fish in an aquarium does it for others. Ponder about how you can get to that space and do it for some time every single day.

Grace does not need me to shake one more rattle or set off a noisier toy that shakes, wiggles, or claps. She needs me to tune into her discomfort and help her get quiet on the inside.

It is a precious lesson that she teaches me. The road to clarity is found by tuning out the world's soundtrack and tuning into my own still small inner voice. That is where true comfort and real answers live.

Turn Off, Tune In

1. Spend three hours away from all your devices—cell phone, TV, iPad, laptop, etc.
2. Use this free time in a different way—just know that it is quiet time, so engage in some contemplative state of beingness.
3. At the end of those three hours, journal about this experience. Identify how disconnecting from your devices felt in your body, mind, and spirit. If you experienced discomfort, reflect on its root. What did this experiment teach you about yourself?

Chapter 9

I'm All about Connection

Cuddle a baby, and they cuddle right back. Coo to a baby, and they babble back. Tickle the soles of their feet, and they gurgle, giggle, and wriggle in your arms.

Seven-month-old Grace even cups my chin with her toothless gums to deliver a wet, sloppy kiss of deep affection. Babies are social animals. Connection is oxygen to them. It's how they thrive. Touching a baby, talking to them, holding them close, or nuzzling their neck are ways in which we help them to thrive.

Michael Mendizza says in his article, 'Intimate body contact, breast feeding, being held, movement and affectionate play provide naturally a constant source of multi-sensory experiences that feed development. From this point of view not breastfeeding, no skin to skin contact, not being held, not moving and playing affectionately are forms of sensory deprivation, which are as damaging as a steady diet of junk food would be or no sunlight to a very new and rapidly developing human being.'[2]

I did a volunteering stint at an orphanage in India where my job was to hold babies who didn't receive enough touch therapy. It started with a visit to the orphanage to donate baby lotion, oil, bottles of formula, and clothes. As I cradled the newborns in my arms, I felt an undeniable tug. Soon, I started to volunteer regularly. Volunteers at the facility were so valued because an array of overwhelmed *ayahs* were doing the best they could to cope with the functional demands of the wailing newborns: changing diapers, bathing them, and sticking to feeding schedules. No sooner than an ayah had cuddled a baby, quieted them down, and lay them down in a crib, the wailing would start again.

Like all babies, Grace loved to snuggle and sleep in my arms. She has napped for as long as three hours in my arms. Twenty minutes into her nap, I would lay her down in her crib, convinced that she was fast asleep. No matter how gently I did this, she would instantly miss the warmth of my arms, wake up, and bawl her protest.

As Grace's nanny, it was hard to even take a bathroom break on the job. As soon as she learned how to crawl, she would follow me into the kitchen when I was making a cup of tea or down the hallway, into the nursery, where I had gone to fetch baby wipes.

Babies love people. It is as simple as that. There is no such thing as a baby who is a 'loner' or 'needs their space'. No baby is born an island.

None of us was born that way.

As babies, we come into the world seeking connection in the most intimate, nurturing way. We trust with an endearing openness and a desire to engage.

Difficult life experiences teach us the art of disengagement. Growing into our teens and early adulthood, life throws challenging people and situations at us, and we cope by building walls we feel safe within. Many of us who were bullied, ridiculed, or humiliated developed negative self-talk and self-beliefs that strengthened over time. We told ourselves that we were not worthy of companionship because nobody liked us. We weren't cool, hip, and popular like others—the guys and girls who always got the hot dates and hero status.

Shamed, we pulled away, withdrew, and hid more and more of ourselves. We donned masks. Over time, it just became a part of who we were. We forgot the real us and became more of the mask. It is socially acceptable to label this kind of person an introvert, wallflower, or private. It is possible to isolate under this guise. Although, not all introverts are disengaged people. Some people prefer their own company and thrive on solitude. Drained by crowds and company, they need alone-time to recharge their batteries.

I have had my share of struggles with lack of connection. When I was sixteen and my family had just moved to a new city, my father, who firmly believed in the value of a good education, picked the best school for me. However, the 'best school' also happened to be the one all the rich kids went to. They arrived in fancy chauffeur-driven cars with branded backpacks and snazzy lunch boxes. I travelled to school in a battered share taxi, a regular yellow cab that a bunch of kids who lived in the same apartment building car pooled in. My lunch was spicy, smelly South Indian food, whereas other kids brought exotic fare like cheese and crackers, sandwiches cut in perfect triangles, and home-baked cookies. It was a world I just didn't fit into because it mocked me and shamed my middle-class origins. Where my father marvelled at the possibility of a stellar academic experience with teachers who spoke in crisp British accents, I experienced the pain of living in the shadows and feeling invisible. I have always loved people but feeling like a poor kid in a rich school during my awkward teenage years caused my self-esteem to plummet to my ankles. I hardly spoke a word to anyone except a girl named Anna who told me I had nice eyes. My humiliation caused me to hide, and I was happy to be left alone.

My college years were a time of healing for me. I loved English and Psychology, subjects I could finally study to my heart's content without the must-do of Math and Science, subjects I had zero skill in. Analysing poetry and writing compelling essays came easily to me. All of a sudden, the doors to appreciation and accolades opened up. I was valued and liked. I did well in academics and was recognised by my professors. To know and accept that I had value dissolved some of the pain. Connection made it possible for me to ease my way back to the world of friendships.

We yearn for connection. We long for a sense of belonging. But when the world shoots too many arrows in our direction, we fend off the attacks by defending and protecting. We push back when people try to get close. We yearn to share our lonely burdens but don't find the kind of people who validate us. So, we eat our loneliness away with a carton of Ben & Jerry's Triple Fudge Sundae, binge on TV shows, or develop the safe-yet-disengaged connection provided by social media.

When we don't allow ourselves to be vulnerable, intimacy is the first casualty. It is hard to cry when you don't know how to. It is a tall order to share your feelings when you have been taught not to show them. But vulnerability is a great connector; it is what opens our hearts to each other and lets us love. Brené Brown, research professor at the University of Houston and author of *The Gifts of Imperfection: Let Go of Who You Think You're Supposed to Be and Embrace Who You Are*, says: 'Heroics is often about putting our life on the line. Ordinary courage is about putting our vulnerability on the line. In today's world, that's pretty extraordinary.'[3]

The lack of vulnerability leaves us lonely. As an epidemic that plagues the West, loneliness seems to be right up there with rape, diabetes, heart disease, and obesity. We have lost the art of connection; we have become guarded and suspicious. We navigate our life by trying to protect our gaping wounds from other wounded humans.

We crave companionship, but when we send out strong self-sufficiency vibes, we scare others off. This has been a cultural struggle for me. Raised in a culture that values connection, I grew up seeing our neighbour, Auntie Rose, walk across the fence holding out an empty sugar bowl and say to my mother, 'Lakshmi, here I am with my begging bowl.' My mother would top up her sugar bowl instantly, and the two of them would share a coffee at our dining table and trade family stories like they had all the time in the world. Apparently, they did.

I had to come to an understanding that self-reliance is a cherished value to people in the West—even to the extent that they fend off assistance when they need it. In India, it was common for me to carry an elder's grocery bags, vacate my seat in an auditorium, or rush to pick up something they had accidentally dropped. This is a deeply ingrained habit, one I instinctively resorted to in the retirement community where I found employment when we moved to Chicago. For the longest time, I didn't understand the refusals that came my way, the looks of scorn, and the emphatically voiced: 'I can get it.' Behaviour, for which I was usually rewarded with a blessing or a grateful smile, now made people mad. It was a while before I understood that my assistance was an affront to the American seniors' independence, a highly prized virtue in this part of the world. To this day, I struggle with the reality of men and women in their seventies and eighties shovelling snow, lugging heavy bags of groceries, and negotiating stairs as they live alone in apartments.

In our tech-obsessed world, virtual communities of communication and connection abound. People chat on screens and share anniversary and family reunion pictures via Facebook and Instagram. A chance conversation with a neighbour working in their yard or throwing a ball to their dog—an opportunity for conversation and camaraderie in small-town America—is fenced off. We are more comfortable texting than talking on the phone.

Weighed down by this baggage, we often enter the intimate territory of marriage with little practice on how to give and take. It is all too easy to get mired in a power struggle. Clearly, we have minimal understanding of how to ask and receive graciously.

Babies, on the other hand, are open and engaging. They have no walls. They are simply unaware of comparisons and have no judgments about self-worth. They are the happiest when they are with pets and people they know. In the absence of a history of interaction, they only see the goodness in others and connect instinctively.

When I babble at Grace, she flashes me the most wonderful toothless smile, as if to say: 'Keep talking; I'm listening because I feel the love in your voice even if I don't understand your words. It lets me know that I'm loved.'

So, we talk the hours away and hug and cuddle and kiss. My baby girl teaches me the true joy in connection— when we engage with no agendas.

Seek Connection

1. The next time you are in a store, make eye contact with the cashier.
2. Ask them a question about how their day is going.
3. Really listen with all of you. Even if they respond in monosyllables, see if you can pay them a compliment.
4. Value that moment of connection.

Chapter 10

I Communicate What I'm Feeling

A dry diaper and a belly full of milk is heaven for a baby. Well, most of the time. As a provider of those basic comforts, I get to experience a little bit of that heaven in the heart-warming smile Grace beams my way.

Equally, Grace lets me know when matters are otherwise. When she gets fussy, I could wave a gazillion distractions in the form of toys that flash lights and beep and sing and bounce. But she will have none of it. She wants me to hear what she is communicating, loud and clear—whether she needs a nap or a cuddle or if she is just not feeling good.

Babies and toddlers are transparent when it comes to feelings. No wonder a toddler in temper-tantrum mode is a supermarket-shopper mom's worst nightmare. Toddlers simply don't care where you are or what your etiquette preferences are.

Babies let us know when something is not right. For instance, the chilly discomfort of sockless feet or when something is enjoyable and fun, like the absurdly silly face or curious sound I make that elicit the most infectious chuckles from Grace.

Babies don't label feelings as good, bad, unacceptable, scary, or risky. They simply feel whatever bubbles up to the surface. A scary cry when confronted by a loud noise, a hurt cry when an adult says a stern 'No', an angry cry when a bottle of formula is delayed, or a cuddle-me cry when they seek reassurance.

As we lose the natural instincts of childhood and mould our behaviour to what society deems proper, we lose the spontaneity of expression—feelings included. We shut down parts of ourselves that are unacceptable. For decades, I had a hard time accepting the part of me that experienced shame growing up in an alcoholic home. I put on my happy face before I went to school and cried on the inside as I listened to my friends' stories of wonderful weekends that they experienced. I never invited a friend home, terrified that my father would stumble into our midst piss-drunk and shatter my carefully crafted illusion of a happy family. It took years of inner work and self-realisation to accept that I didn't create my drunk father, nor did I have to assume responsibility for his misdemeanours.

But there was a gift in this dismal reality. My mother, three siblings, and I were tightly bonded in our sorrow; conversations and comfort drew us together. It was okay to cry and rage and express whatever emotions swirled within us. We held space for each other on this wobbly raft we called our family as the storm of my father's alcoholism blew around us.

Not everyone is as fortunate. I know from the clients I work with that some people were raised in homes where to speak ill of a family member was blasphemy, no matter the seriousness of their offense. Crying and expressing emotions invited the wrath of authority figures. If you receive a hateful look instead of a handkerchief in response to your tears, you learn very quickly, to swallow your sorrow and work your way through life dry-eyed. There are those who never speak of grief or loss but simply shrug it off. On the other hand, anger is mostly accepted because it is about injustice and seems to be the major currency of tolerable emotional expression. To say, 'I hate the way he speaks to me' is acceptable. On the other hand, 'I'm scared to disagree with my friend or I might lose her friendship' is not.

Hurt and fear are mostly disguised as anger or feelings of superiority. Masks and walls become comfortable armour. The mask is about pretending, and the wall is about defending. As we grow older, the masks mesh with our very skin and the walls grow thicker and more impenetrable. Ensconced in its safe confines, we move through life believing that we must hide those aspects of our personality that may invite judgment. To be judged is to be excluded, and to be excluded is to feel disconnected and alone. So, we suck it up and soldier on.

When we run into a friend or an acquaintance and exchange the common greeting of 'Hey, how are you doing?', our reflexive response is, 'I'm good!' I am not always feeling 'good' when asked this question, but the word rolls off my tongue with practiced ease. Sometimes, I wish I could say, 'I'm frustrated right now because I had an argument with . . .' or 'I have been somewhat sad because I miss my sister in India. It is hard to be so far away.'

What stops me from verbalising my feelings? The conviction that no one has the time or the inclination to listen, no one really wants to know, and no one cares about my feelings when they are dealing with their own stuff. And so, it is easier to package it all in a single-syllable and easy-to-swallow 'good'. It is a civil exchange where I cause no discomfort to the other, and they feel safe enough to ask me the question again in a future encounter because I didn't throw them off with a sentimental saga. Do I have all the time in the world to spare a listening ear to every sad story that comes my way? Perhaps not. Sometimes, it is easier not to invite a confession and feel the obligation to stay and listen.

In an effort to present a strong front to the world, we only show feelings that are acceptable. Tears are perceived as a sign of weakness. To admit to fear triggers our shame and inadequacy. The sadness of grief is pushed away with prescription meds or buried in frenetic work schedules. We long to bond with fellow humans and share our journey, yet we hang back and hesitate to reach out, lest we are rejected.

Whether we are junking on work, food, alcohol, drugs, or the Internet, as a species, we have become addicted to numbing our feelings. Pushing away unpleasant feelings is all too easy in the era of *iNumb* that we live in. Celebrity struggles and reality television serve as happy distractions from our own dramas. Cell phones and tablets have become escape gadgets that we use to plot our getaways via a maze of cyber trails. We trade our real, emotional identities for the seduction of digital magic. Communicating digitally is easier than face-to-face encounters where body language betrays our truth. When you look someone in the eye and speak your mind, it requires a level of honesty and vulnerability that can make you feel naked. It is so much easier to be invisible and bare your shame to a stranger through a chat room, halfway across the world, whose identity is MonkeyMind622. In our increasingly digital world, we have become more comfortable talking to automated voices, engaging with mechanised checkouts, and ordering our favourite foods in a restaurant with an iPad or Android menu.

Technology definitely has its upside. Using WhatsApp on my cell phone, I can ask my sister, who lives in Mumbai (India), what she cooked for dinner or get to know how she is feeling about a difficult domestic situation. It's pure joy to watch an eighty-five-year-old woman's face light up as she sees and hears her newborn great-grandchild on Skype. I have friends in countries, the names of which I can barely pronounce, thanks to Facebook and we collaborate to do programs and interviews that serve our clients globally.

But technology cannot hold my hand when I cry. To be human is to feel. Our feelings exist for a reason. They serve as a radar to help us negotiate our physical world. Feelings are felt in the body as sensations. If we learn how to drop into our bodies often enough, we would learn to recognise its warning, either to not take a particular course of action or to follow the joy of an opportunity that is right for us. The prickly sensation we experience when we are around someone is our body's way of letting us know that there is something about them we need to pay attention to. Sometimes, the sick sensation in the pit of our stomach is how we know that we are making the wrong choice. We ignore the signals because we have been conditioned to think things through, not feel them.

As adults, we categorise experiences as pleasurable and painful. We want more of the fun, feel-good variety of experiences that give us a serotonin rush, and we do all we can to steer clear of situations and feelings that are likely to cause us pain.

Feelings are the language of the soul and they were given to guide us on the human journey. In a world that celebrates logic and the left brain, the wisdom of the heart is sadly overlooked. Is it any wonder that we have forgotten how to feel? On the occasions when I have felt hurt because of an insensitive remark that came my way, I have tried to brush it off for fear of being branded 'sensitive'. But in the instances when I have allowed myself a good cry and washed my soul clean, I have felt peace flow into me. The release of that emotional energy does me a world of good.

Babies are natural feelers. Grace does not enjoy waking up in a dark room. So, she cries and lets me know what she is feeling. Maybe, she is scared, or she feels alone and sad at the fact that the adults she loves and trusts are nowhere near her. She feels something, and she lets me know. She also reminds me that I can find a trusted friend to talk to when I am sad instead of pretending that all is well or posting a status update on Facebook.

Let us take a leaf out of a baby's book. They know what is good for them . . . and for all of us.

Feel Your Feelings

1. Close your eyes and recall a sad event.
2. Without any judgment, allow the feelings to rise within you—whether it is tears, aloneness, or anger.

3. Be with the feelings. Stay even when you are tempted to distract yourself, or worse, run away.
4. Ask what you are afraid of, what the sadness is about, or what hides beneath your anger.
5. Feel the energy of that emotion move through and out of you when you stay present to feeling it.

Chapter 11

I Am Beauty

Grace is the prettiest, cutest, most adorable baby in my world. The beauty is that she doesn't know it. She has no clue that she has the most gorgeous silken hair, hazel eyes that sparkle with mischief and delight, satiny soft skin, and a million-megawatt smile that can melt the sternest heart. Grace has no sense of self. What a wonderful place to be!

She looks beautiful no matter what she is wearing, and all I want to do is scoop her up in my arms and smother her with kisses. Saffron and burgundy were made for her, pastels and floral prints are elevated by her, and she looks just as adorable when she is wearing nothing but a humble Huggies.

But it is not only her ginger hair or creamy skin that make Grace beautiful. Her beauty is the essence of her sweet self.

What of those babies who are born with deformities—a misshapen nose or a cleft lip? Being pure consciousness, they don't know how to be less than whole. This state of not-knowing is part of their radiance. It is their parents who suffer the heartbreak knowing that challenges will follow their child; a child who must grow up different in a world that thrives on the competitive edge, where judgments around external appearances are painfully real. However, if you watch a brown-skinned toddler building a tower of blocks with a Caucasian toddler, they don't see themselves as different from the other, and there are no value judgments based on appearances.

The cute factor in babies is irresistible (at least for baby lovers like me), and we are drawn to babies not only because of their beauty, but also their purity. We are attracted to their essence, the wholeness and loveliness that springs from a place deep within.

Grace doesn't think about degrees of beauty because she does not know herself as a separate self. Not yet, at least. She is still untouched by the conditioning that attaches value to looks.

As we start growing into an awareness of who is beautiful and not, our world becomes crowded with comparisons. Teen years are a nightmare; everything hinges on the shape of one's nose, size of one's thighs, and the span of one's pectoral muscles. Growing into adulthood, most of us go through a period of severe judgment about our physical beauty, or the lack of it.

During my teenage years, I was extremely conscious of my lanky and brown-skinned self. I could perceive no aspect of beauty in myself and tried to fade into the background as much as possible. I didn't have any of the prized attributes of young South Indian girls—thick, long braids, flawless cappuccino skin, or the grace and agility of a well-proportioned physique. When I looked in the mirror, I saw someone who was too dark, too skinny, and too asymmetrical. It was a severe crisis of confidence, one that I overcame only in my mid-twenties. Able assistance from home-made herbal remedies to banish acne helped, as did friendly salons who helped shape my meagre tresses, and the welcome extra pounds I forced myself to gain. I am not even going to get into the problem the pounds represent now!

It is true that a lot of time is wasted in taking an inventory of all that is not right with us. It seems to be a rite of passage that every young person must go through because we have come to believe that we are defined by our looks and shape. Either my nose is too flat, or my eyes are too deep, or my lips are too thick—so I must be less than.

It is part of our relentless quest for perfection. We live in a culture that celebrates the perfect curves and tight skin of youth. Often, what is on the outside is more valued than what is on the inside. Chinese and Korean girls aspire for almond eyes and seek plastic surgery to make their dreams come true. Matrimonial advertisements in Indian newspapers and websites declare a preference for fair-skinned brides. White-skinned women fork out hundreds of dollars at tanning salons for the coveted bronze look, and African-American women, often, readily exchange their tight curls for a curtain of straight blonde hair.

We come into the world as whole, perfect beings, get stomped on by imperfect people, and, then, begin to seek perfection. The voices of our parents, teachers, priests, and other authority figures become our own and take up residence inside our heads. These voices erode our self-esteem and convince us of our fundamental flaws by drawing attention to them time and again.

Of the seven billion people on the planet, there is only one of you. It is a staggering statistic when you ponder the implications. Yet, we spend a good part of our lives trying and wanting to be someone else.

Women bemoan the onset of the menopausal years as the period from where 'everything starts to go downhill'. Christiane Northrup, an ob-gyn and well-known author, attempts to address the issue of ageing and the terror about the appearance of wrinkles that herald the end of beauty in her latest book, *Goddesses Never Age: The Secret Prescription for Radiance, Vitality, and Well-Being*. One of her quotes on Facebook says: 'Cosmetic surgery won't heal your life or your relationship with your body, but it may very well enhance your experience of looking at yourself in the mirror.'

I remember an episode of *The Oprah Winfrey Show* that featured twenty-eight-year-old Jenny Lee who had undergone twenty-six plastic surgeries in pursuit of the perfect nose, breasts, thighs, tummy, and face. When she stood in front of the mirror, she only saw her imperfections and continued to go after a series of fixes in the hope that the next surgery would accomplish her magical transformation. Slave to the scalpel and several thousand dollars poorer, she was in tears as she confessed to Oprah that she still didn't feel beautiful. She was trying so hard to fix on the outside what was essentially an inner landscaping job.

Another guest on the show, who had a profoundly powerful impact on me, was the young and beautiful Jacqui Saburido. A twenty-year-old Venezuelan who relocated to Texas to learn English, Jacqui was badly burned in a car crash that involved a drunk driver. Her face, hair, and skin literally melted in the accident, and she had to endure over fifty surgeries at the end of which she was left with a hideous face. But her inner beauty shone through so brightly as she said, 'I'm still the same person on the inside. I feel beautiful.' She refused to label the young man whose actions had dramatically altered the course of her destiny forever. She believed that his intentions were not irresponsible, and she would not name him a 'criminal'. To me, that kind of beauty is very rare.

If sixteen-year-old Grace came to me, and said, 'I don't feel beautiful. I don't think I'm pretty', I would gather her in my arms and swiftly dispel the notion with reassurances. 'Honey', I would say, 'your beauty shines from inside. Let no one tell you otherwise.' But we seldom address the little girl or boy aching for some affection inside us. Instead, we beat up on them. Embracing and loving ourselves is one of the hardest assignments in this earthly incarnation. If we don't learn how to, we will never get off the tiring spiral of approval-seeking, aping, and measuring our self-worth by others' standards.

'We mistake glamour for beauty', says Irish poet, priest, author, and philosopher, John O'Donohue. 'We do live in a culture which is very addicted to the image . . . there is always an uncanny symmetry between the way you are inward and the way you are outward.'[4] To me, the soul is all about symmetry. What is on the inside—whether it is bitterness, anxiety, or self-hatred—is what is reflected on the outside. Equally, one's inner radiance cannot be hidden, for it shines forth. We feel the beauty of such people when we are in their presence.

Nature and animals are great teachers of this lesson. The oak tree is content because it is not trying to be a mango tree or a papaya tree. The rose never compares and judges its shades with tulips and dahlias. The cocker spaniel is happy to be one, he doesn't ever crave to look like a Doberman.

I know in the deepest part of my being that internal beauty has very little to do with physical attributes or assets. I have known people with flat noses or chunky thighs or misshapen feet to be some of the most beautiful souls I have encountered. In fact, it is their confidence, despite their imperfect attributes, that makes them so attractive. I am drawn to them because their attractiveness is about their aura. It is a magnetic pull that makes me want to be in their space and imbibe some of their sublime quality.

Jacqui Saburido says, 'I allow myself five minutes to cry when I'm having a really bad day.' Then, she snaps out of it and tries to be grateful for all her blessings.

Beauty and ugliness exist within all of us.
The divine and the devil.
Light and shadow.
Sacred and the profane.

While babies with their brand-new skin and life are undeniably adorable, there is also a soul light that shines bright in those nearing the end of their lives. I have seen this light and been awed by it. It is almost as if this light shines bright one last time before the soul takes off to God knows where.

Instead of obsessing about 'Am I beautiful?' it may be a better idea to phrase the question as 'What beauty is mine to express?' This idea was introduced by a beloved teacher of mine, Janet Conner, who guides her students to a more expansive definition of beauty. The truth is—we all have beautiful gifts that are uniquely ours to express. If we allowed our souls to sing our song, our expressions would blossom and bring joy to the world.

When asked what images came to mind when he thought of beauty, John O'Donohue responded, 'When I think of the word "beauty", some of the faces of those that I love come into my mind . . . Then I think of acts of such lovely kindness that have been done to me by people that cared for me in bleak, unsheltered times or when I needed to be loved and minded. . . . I think of music. . . . I think of beauty in poetry.'[5]

I think we are most beautiful when we express our inner gifts. Grace, like all wise babies, knows and lives by this truth. She radiates a beautiful aura of purity and gentleness and absolute, perfect love.

Our beauty is lit up by our very essence, the core of who we are. Comparing ourselves with others is an exercise in frustration, fuel for unfulfillment.

Grace teaches me this profound yet simple truth, simply by being who she is.

Find the Beauty

1. The next time you are challenged by a co-worker, friend, or your spouse, pause and tune into some aspect, any aspect of their beauty. It could be the shape of their fingers, the way they balance a chequebook, the care with which they arrange flowers, or the colour of their eyes.
2. Try to find something of beauty in everyone you meet, no matter how morose or awkward or withdrawn they may be.

3. If you are struggling to find this aspect,
    remind yourself of the soul light that remains
    hidden behind their painful persona.

Chapter 12

I Don't Have an Ego (Not Yet)

A baby has no sense of 'I', 'me', or 'my'. There is a complete absence of self-identity. Watch a baby interact with others, their toys, and even themselves, and you will see evidence of this truth. Grace doesn't know where 'she' ends and 'the other' begins. If I plucked a rattle out of her hand, she would simply turn her attention to the next thing in her world. No argument, no protest. Whether I change her diaper or the next-door neighbour does, she doesn't care as long as she gets a fresh diaper at the end of it. If she is fussy but has to wait a while for me to pick her up and rock her to sleep, she doesn't hold it against me.

As a baby grows into toddlerhood, the process of separation begins and the chasm between *self* and *other* grows. The first signs of the ego-self appear when the toddler learns about possessions: my toys versus Shan's toys. Until that time, a baby lives in a world of no separation. All things are connected and there is a sense of peaceful oneness, a happy coexistence with everyone and everything.

Ego separation is a necessary conduit to our self-identity; it is an important ally on the human journey. But the trouble begins when we allow the ego to lead.

Once it is behind the wheel of our life, it quickly turns saboteur. The ego is most useful when it is in the passenger seat.

The ego lives in fear. It believes that if someone else gets more, it will end up with less. When this competitive and defensive stance causes disconnection, it can potentially shut a human being down. As adults, we become more and more disengaged from the knowing that we are all connected as spiritual beings. Singer and songwriter Jana Stanfield's lyrics convey this truth beautifully: '*You cry just like me; I hurt just like you.*' We are on the same human journey, just walking different paths. We need each other, but we would rather not accept that reality. As spiritual teacher and author, Ram Dass, says so well: 'We're all just walking each other home.'

Interconnectedness is the primary structure of our physical universe. The web of life weaves together just as our ears, toes, nose, kidneys, and bones are all interconnected and serve one common goal—to support the body's well-being.

It is easy to forget this wonderful premise when we are trapped in the ceaseless chatter of the monkey mind. We need the mind because human thought is a tool for organising and categorising. But when we use thought to divide and separate, we experience disconnection. If I have a need to feel superior, I must make someone feel inferior. If I am attached to my religious beliefs as a Hindu, I must, somehow, find a way to make Muslims wrong.

The ego's mantra is *more*. If I have more—possessions, status, and accolades—and *do* more—successful, ambitious, and driven—I am more; I have increased value and worth. Human beings are the only species that subscribe to this idea because we have a mind which gives birth to ideas, opinions, and judgments. This is where separation takes root.

Nature thrives on the power of interconnectedness. Trees provide oxygen and shelter for us, and we make carbon dioxide—an important greenhouse gas—in grateful exchange. Bees travel from flower to flower for sustenance and scatter pollen for new growth. Clouds transform into rain which nourishes the earth's soil and trees, and the water evaporates and forms more clouds.

The Vietnamese Buddhist monk, Thich Nhat Hanh, explains this sense of interdependence in a simple yet profound way. A sheet of paper, he says, contains everything—from clouds to sunshine, rain, and soil. He traces it to the cloud that made the rain that nourished the tree which flourished in the sunlight and, in turn, produced the paper we hold in our hands.[6]

It is, often, too easy to lose sight of this sense of connectedness in intimate relationships. I am certainly guilty of it. Caught up in the rights and wrongs of a situation, I create a mental divide. Often, an argument with my husband escalates to the point where we become competitors instead of teammates. Minutes into the situation, there are fences and judgments about who is right and wrong. In this state, it becomes easy to stick labels—aggressive, argumentative, or critical—on the other person.

Agreed, we are all unique personalities. But I am not always able to stay connected to the truth that beneath the layer of personality is a God spark—our soul. Our personality is merely an earthly garb for our spirit.

It is so easy to compare and differentiate on the basis of gender, race, religious and political affiliation, economic status, sexual orientation, and educational background. I think of the truth that a hero and a hobo will, eventually, come down to the same level: a plot of land under the earth.

As long as we remain attached to how different we are, we cannot step into the territory of oneness. I need you, and you need me. We are meant to assist each other. We are made for community, not isolation. The more we connect and share, the more joyful our lives will be.

'Babies come into this world trailing the breath of angels,' says Oprah Winfrey. Pure and untainted by worldliness, they are instinctive about their divine origin. In their pure egoless state, they are the best teachers of the truth—our souls can be enslaved by our ego, or our ego can be in service to our souls. It is our choice.

The Voice of Spirit

1. When you are in the midst of a challenge and your monkey mind is up to its tricks, take a moment's conscious pause.
2. Listen to the voices. Separate the voice of ego from the voice of Spirit. The ego always reminds you of your fears and inadequacies. The voice of Spirit is always infused with love.
3. Now, ask yourself the question: 'What would the loving voice of Spirit say?'

Chapter 13

I LOVE TO LEARN

A baby is all about possibility. If they didn't arrive into this world with curiosity and possibility built into them, they would learn nothing. Babies have to challenge themselves constantly to reach developmental milestones. Being in the delightful space of 'zero experience', they apply their innate intelligence in unique ways to master and navigate their ever-expanding Universe.

Grace is almost one. Amongst her impressive assortment of toys is a pink elephant with its trunk pointed upwards. The elephant has a slide on its side. When you feed small, coloured balls down this slide and push a button, the trunk sucks the balls up so that they pop out into the air almost magically.

Unable to comprehend or question the principle of this operation, Grace simply decided to have fun with it. Tired of pushing the balls down the slide, one day, she decided to experiment with her wooden blocks. The density of the wooden blocks prevented them from being sucked up to the surface like the tiny balls. But my little Gracie didn't know that. She peered into the elephant's trunk with the eager anticipation that comes so easily to kids. When the blocks didn't pop up magically like the balls had, she decided to repeat the process with a few green apple slices left over from her breakfast. Over the following weeks, I was constantly called upon to rescue Cheddar puffs, dog food, and the remains of a squished banana from the poor elephant's trunk.

Fun with experimentation is, often, the best way to learn something, anything. What drove Grace to experiment in this fashion was a simple question of 'what if'. She didn't know those words, but she came into this world with the what-if gene built into her, the gene all babies are born with, the gene you and I were born with.

Grace and the pink elephant reminded me that it is only possible to exist in the space of possibility if we are open to new ideas, new learning, and new ways of doing things. It is precisely because babies and toddlers live in this realm that they are fascinated by almost everything in the world.

Visualise a kindergarten classroom when the teacher asks a question. Tiny hands shoot up in the air, eager to respond. Now, visualise a high-school classroom when the teacher asks a question. It takes a while for the room to warm up, and, then, a few tentative hands go up. Young kids are not attached to the idea of being right. They don't care about mistakes because mistakes don't define them. Teenagers and adults are more invested in being right and knowing the correct answer. Scarred by ridicule from peers and parents and the pressure to perform well, we have learned that it is safer to be silent when we are unsure.

Being the brightest and the best has traditionally been more about who knows the answer. How much better it would be if we commended those who ask the best questions or exhibit the greatest curiosity? Learning is, by definition, knowledge that is taught, acquired through experience or study. Knowing alone does not guarantee success. Trying out anything new—whether it is an idea, a behaviour, or a skill—includes the process of not getting it right the first time. Those who strongly identify with their skills and are attached to their level of competence may struggle to adopt a new method which requires them to do something in an unfamiliar way.

Like most people, I, too, am attached to the boundaries of my comfort zone. I struggle through healthy doses of trepidation when I embark on learning something new that pushes me into the space of the unfamiliar. Perhaps, the biggest leap into the great unknown came in April 2008 when my husband, teen daughter, and I left the Indian subcontinent to begin a new life in America. Friends and family warned us that we were uprooting our teen at a vulnerable time in her life. My husband and I were in our forties and living a very comfortable life in Chennai, India.

My husband's sister had started the process of helping us immigrate almost fifteen years prior. After the early months and years of anxiously awaiting any piece of mail from the US Consulate, hope had leached away, and we had forgotten about it. Fifteen years later, the Consulate sent a barrage of paperwork our way. Our green cards landed in our laps in a matter of months and we had to decide. Do we go, or do we stay?

What made our decision easier was the fact that my husband's company was willing to find him a position in Chicago. We decided to take the plunge and embarked on our grand adventure.

Learning to navigate a new country and culture challenged us. Getting my driver's license at age forty-four and learning to drive was a huge test for a geographically challenged me. I am not one who dives into an adventure with both feet; I do it with a pounding heart. I am comforted by routine. A life without structure would drive me crazy. But I have discovered that when I push through the discomfort, each new milestone brings growth, expansion, and confidence.

Swiping a credit card at a store was another new trick that I had to learn when we moved from India, something that caused quite a few awkward moments both for me and the checkout clerk.

I also had to master new skills like navigating technology to teach webinars and online courses. It has its frustrating and challenging moments. Once, I pushed the wrong button and deleted an entire presentation. One other time, I muted all the participants, and no one was able to join the Q&A session. But teaching with New Age technology, that can be accessed by people all over the world—New Zealand, Australia, India, and the Netherlands—has been a very exciting experience.

Change is the only constant on the human journey. It is packaged differently for each of us, but it comes when it is supposed to. And when it does, we have to learn a new way of being and doing.

A favourite saying of mine is: 'When you're green, you're growing. When you're ripe, you rot.' Those who think they know it all, resist new ideas and different points of view. If we live in our ivory towers and feel threatened by the smallest change to the way we think or do something, we stagnate.

People we love will die. We may lose a limb or a relationship. We may find ourselves in the middle of a country and culture we know very little about and will be forced to adapt. Marriages run into rough weather. Kids test us in ways we never see coming.

Change, change, change.

American author, editor, and public speaker, Marilyn Ferguson, says: 'It's not so much that we're afraid of change or so in love with the old ways, but it's that place in between that we fear . . . It's like being between trapezes. It's Linus when the blanket is in the dryer. There's nothing to hold on to.'

Every time change is upon us, we are called to learn and modify our behaviour. Being a wordsmith, I enjoy debating an idea, but it has taken me many years to realise that my husband doesn't feel up to competing with me because he sees me as the one with an unfair advantage. I have learned that biting my tongue is a better idea. What I see as engaging wordplay, he sees as one-upmanship even though that, clearly, is not my intent. So, I had to learn a new way of being, in the interests of marital harmony. I have miles to go before I get it right each time because change is hard, even when I know it is good for me.

Grace had to learn to co-ordinate her limbs and eyes so that she could grab hold of the butterfly dangling from her crib. She, then, had to learn how to grasp a rattle in the palm of her hand so that she wouldn't drop it. She also had to learn how to pick up a Cheddar puff and bring it all the way to her mouth in order to taste it.

Learning, learning, learning.

Once, she had learned a new way of doing something, she had to keep repeating it until she could do it effortlessly. And when she did, she didn't have to go back to the old, awkward, and uncomfortable way of doing it.

She evolved to a better way. And that is the purpose of all new learning—evolution.

I saw the most heart-warming example of adult openness to learning on a television show. Viewers were introduced to a 105-year-old woman who was the 'oldest person on Facebook' with over 30,000 friends. When she was ninety-five, her adult children gifted her a laptop, digital camera, and an Internet connection, and she hasn't been the same since. She also volunteers and has been doing so for the past forty years. She writes cards and glues envelopes and has a blast doing it. Going on Facebook and engaging with the world at ninety-five is a great example of a mind that is still curious, alert, and open.

And as for my little toddler, Grace teaches me that it is okay to shove green apple slices into the pink elephant's trunk and watch what happens. She is most definitely the teacher and I, the student. Age has nothing to do with it.

Challenge Yourself

1. If your right hand is your dominant hand, use your left hand to do a few things that you always do with your right.
2. Learn a new language, take a class in something that is outside your comfort zone, or read a thriller if your regular staple is self-help books.
3. Journal about the discomfort as well as the positives of the learning experience. Also jot down the insights you gained from the challenge.

Chapter 14

I LOVE GROWING OLDER

Babies have no concept of time or space, so they live happily in the now. When it is time to crawl, they crawl; when it is time to teethe, they teethe; when it is time to sit, they sit. As weeks roll into months, they arrive at each new milestone, flowing in sync with their inner programming.

I remember the days when Grace was transitioning from a crawler to a stander-upper. She had reached the stage of the downward dog yoga pose and continued to practice it for weeks. Finally, there came a day when she let go of her hands, pushed herself up tentatively, and beamed a big smile when she finally stood on her own two feet. Every time she performed this feat—standing up without holding on to the coffee table or the leg of an armchair—out came the megawatt smile of triumph.

Every ounce of her being focused on perfecting the art of standing. Within days, not only did she stand, she began to toddle all over the house. Her initial attempts were clumsy; there were many butt landings, thankfully cushioned by a well-padded diaper, but her balance improved all the time.

Next, she mastered the art of climbing. This required more co-ordination and muscle strength and took longer to achieve. But once she had perfected it, the dining table, couches, and the master bed morphed into delightful mountains.

Where am I going with this? Once Grace knew how to stand, she had no desire to go back to crawling. Once she was able to climb, she no longer thought walking was the pinnacle of mobility. With each stage, she was moving towards the next target she could master.

Remember those childhood days when we could hardly wait for our next birthday because it meant we would be a whole year older? We didn't care two hoots about the chronology. Being a year older meant being able to do more, be more, and have more. It meant earning privileges our annoying big brother or sister had already earned simply because they were ahead of us in time.

For a kid, growing older means more choices, more freedom, and more independence. For adults, growing older, sometimes, means fewer choices, less freedom, and a contraction of independence. Every senior I have known in my nine years in America bemoans the driver's license they had to give up. Every one of them laments having had to give up their home, garden, and neighbourhood for a tiny apartment in senior living with a lifetime of possessions sentimentally stowed in storage.

It is one thing when octogenarians and nonagenarians struggle with ageing. But I am both amused and astounded when thirty-somethings talk about a fortieth birthday being the beginning of 'going downhill'. Their talk suggests that their best days are well behind them. In a game show I recently watched, the host asked the question: 'Which is the birthday adults dread the most?'

Forty was the correct answer. One only has to count the number of anti-ageing cream commercials on television and this truth bears out. Lotions and potions with the promise of age reversal and ever-youthful skin are now a coveted part of many women's beauty regimen.

Ageing is a bad word in America. We go from not talking about it to a mild panic attack when early wrinkles present themselves. With the onset of retirement, baby boomers and GenXers, as they are fashionably called, become aware that their world shrinks a little more. They become hyperaware when a few nights out leave them fatigued.

True expansion of the soul can only come from living and struggling and triumphing over life's hurdles over seven or eight decades. The richness of the harvest can only be experienced if we have lived through the springs and summers of life, gathering life experiences like fodder for the winters of our life. Growing old is inevitable; ageing gracefully is optional. Some of the most valuable lessons in ageing come to me from the seniors I work with. Those who grumble and groan about every conceivable thing in their lives are the ones who hate where they are on the chronology scale. Those who meet their days with a sense of purpose and meaning look at age as just a number. They are not defined by their greys or wrinkles and seem to be connected to a larger sense of usefulness. It is not that they have had it easy, but they have tilled the soil of their lives and tended to the unfinished business of their hearts.

I would love to age as gracefully as they have. Like the ninety-two-year-old who still takes a weekly art lesson; the eighty-five-year-old who lost a son forty years ago but speaks of him with such tenderness, her eyes glistening with love. Or the ninety-year-old who wore the tallest heels I have ever seen someone her age wear with outfits co-ordinated with the perfect accessories. They are my heroes and heroines.

Michelangelo was sixty-six when he completed the Last Judgment in the Sistine Chapel, seventy-one when he was named the chief architect of the Vatican, and eighty-nine when he was working on a piece called 'The *Rondanini Pieta*' in the last week of his life.

In many Eastern cultures, ageing is a valued experience. The elderly are regarded as wisdom keepers of the generations. In my own experience growing up in India, I have watched my grandmother who, in her sixties, would consult with her mother when she needed a clarification on customs, rituals, or observance of certain traditions. Likewise, my uncle never failed to consult my grandfather before he made an investment, considered a career change, or shortlisted colleges for his son.

In such cultures, to grow old is to grow in stature. I was taught, at a very young age, not to voice dissension even if I disagreed with an elder. Why wouldn't someone want to grow old in a culture where they accumulate respect with every year added to their age?

I am more of me at fifty-two than I have ever been. I like the skin I am in and follow my passions with joy. I know what truly matters in my life and give my best energies to those pursuits. No longer driven by the need for approval and applause, I am learning every single day to embrace the parts of me that I had pushed away. In my twenties and thirties, the energy that drove me was pure ambition. What drives me today is meaning.

The desire to live a wholesome life, love well, and make a difference in the world gets me out of bed each morning.

Rabbi Zalman Schachter-Shalomi and his co-author, Ronald Miller, sum up this sentiment beautifully in the book, *From Age-Ing to Sage-Ing: A Revolutionary Approach to Growing Older*: 'If we looked back on our lives with complete honesty, many of us would conclude, "I was lived by my parents; I was lived by my teachers; I was lived by society."'[7]

Everything in nature honours the cycle of life. Nature, consistently, reflects the theme of new life, decay, death, and rebirth. The seasons cycle through patiently with gifts they bring us. Spring blossoms followed by hot sunshine, autumn foliage, and the hibernation that comes with winter when the earth sleeps under a blanket of white.

Waking up to stiff joints, being out of breath while taking the stairs, and struggling to maintain balance are not easy to embrace as we age. But ageing can also be a beautiful thing if we make peace with it and allow its fluid grace to influence our rhythm. With age comes wisdom that is born out of life experiences and lessons learned from mistakes and failures. In those who age gracefully, there is a willingness to move with the flow instead of fighting the current. As the great French writer Marcel Proust says, 'The real voyage of discovery consists not in seeking new landscapes, but in having new eyes.' If we can keep our curiosity alive, ageing can be a time of new discovery. After all, we are never too old or young to learn what we don't know.

As Grace flows seamlessly from one milestone to the next, she is not rushing it, nor is she holding back. Her journey is the natural order of things, and she knows it by instinct. So, ageing can be a wise and wonderful journey if we open ourselves up and allow the richness of a ripened life to deliver its essence.

Ageless You

1. Find a comfortable position and close your eyes.
2. Take three deep, slow, and easy breaths.
3. With each inhale and exhale begin to focus on your spirit.
4. Embrace the understanding that your body is animated by your spirit.
5. Anchor in the truth that breath has no age. Your spirit is beyond decay.
6. Always connect with that ageless, timeless part of you when you are trapped in the reality of your body's decline.

Chapter 15

I Focus on One Thing at a Time

If Grace is playing with her shape-sorter and sees me picking up the tiny horse that goes clippety-clop down a pre-fabricated pathway, she drops the shape-sorter and heads for the horse. Now, her attention is totally focused on the horse.

If she is holding a ball in her right hand and a doll in her left, she must let the ball go before she is able to engage with her doll. I have watched her do this over and over with several toys in her chest.

In her right hand is a wooden block. Her eyes land on a teacup from her doll's house and she decides she must have it. Block in right hand; tea cup in left. She looks from one to the other, and then chooses what she will focus on, dropping the non-preferred object to the floor.

A baby's developing brain needs to focus all its attention on one thing at a time.

In the era of modern technology, focus is a scattered word. Like monkeys swinging from one tree limb to another, our attention wavers in distraction mode. Blame it on Bill Gates! He is the one who enabled us to keep several windows open so that we can toggle from task to task. Impatience is the hallmark of the multitasking era. Even as our laptop is starting up, we grab our phone to check if any new emails have arrived.

I miss those days of long, lazy telephone conversations and letter writing. I remember that beautiful instrument called the landline. Those were the days when the boundary of your mobility was the length of the telephone wire, so we gave all of ourselves to the conversation. We either sat down or stood as we talked, so all we did was focus on the conversation. Or we sat and penned a long newsy letter which was the next best thing to the gift of our personal time.

Today, we bow in front of our refrigerator, cell phone tucked between shoulder and ear, trying to decide what to eat for lunch. We push buttons on a microwave, get the coffee-maker going, instruct a team member on a problem at work, throw in wet laundry into the dryer, pet the dog, and pat the kid while talking on our cell phone. No wonder so many of us are exhausted all the time. The brain was clearly not built for such mental gymnastics.

Sometimes, I wish I could peek inside the so-called multitasking brain's frazzled neural circuitry. I imagine it looks like the L.A. freeway in there. The term 'multitasking' was used for decades to describe the parallel processing abilities of computers. This is now shorthand for how humans attempt to do as many things simultaneously as possible, as fast as possible with many different technology aids as possible.

Multitasking has assumed manic proportions in our lives. Women drivers apply mascara and lipstick at traffic signals, people fiddle with their music system and GPS, grab tissues from the glove compartment, sip coffee, and unwrap a sandwich all at the same time. Just writing about it makes me dizzy.

Research shows that our brains are biologically

incapable of processing more than one attention-requiring input at a time.[8] When we think we are multitasking, we are actually shifting attention back and forth, utilising our short-term memory. While the brain can keep track of more than one thing at a time, it cannot actually execute two distinct tasks at once. If two tasks are performed at once, one of the tasks has to be familiar which we can do on autopilot mode while we pay attention to task two. I often listen to a podcast while folding laundry, a perfect example of this theory. I find it calming. Not only does the laundry get done; I have gained a few precious morsels of wisdom doing something that is mundane and domestic.

Researchers David Myer, Jeffrey Evans, and Joshua Rubinstein suggest that productivity can be reduced by as much as 40 per cent due to the mental blocks created when people switch tasks.[9] Of course, that doesn't apply to texting a friend while watching a game. But it could prove to be fatal in a fraction of a second if you are talking on the phone while driving down the highway.

Russell Poldrack, a psychology professor at the University of California, Los Angeles, concludes that multitasking changes the way people learn. He ponders the implications this has for kids and teens whose everyday reality is a media mix: the Internet, video games, text messages, cell phones, and email.[10] We are built to focus, so this frazzled scattering of attention definitely affects our ability to retrieve information. Focusing is becoming a lost art. Many people I know need white noise while they attend to their work, and I know from my college-going daughter that her peers cannot study without earphones plugged into their ears, feeding them a constant stream of music or podcasting.

John Medina, neuroscientist and author, writes, 'Until researchers started measuring the effects of cell phone distractions under controlled conditions, nobody had any idea how profoundly they can impair a driver. It's like driving drunk. Recall that large fractions of a second are consumed every time the brain switches tasks. Cell phone talkers are a half-second slower to hit the brakes in emergencies, slower to return to normal speed after an emergency, and more wild in their "following distance" behind the vehicle in front of them.'[11]

The opposite of multitasking is arguably mindfulness. We live in times when mindfulness is as critical as a seat belt. The core of mindfulness is the ability to pay attention. No matter how much multitasking is valued in our society, the human brain is a sequential processor. Multitasking decreases productivity while increasing the frequency of errors. When there is a space between stimulus and response, we make conscious choices instead of reacting in a knee-jerk fashion.

Kids who are growing up in today's cyber culture are wired to the web. However, rapid-fire processing comes at a cost. When kids multitask, their brains make such quick decisions and respond to stimuli in a way that comprehension and retention are sacrificed.

Researchers at Cornell divided a classroom of students into two groups. One group was allowed online access as they listened to a lecture while the other group was completely unplugged. Whereas the group that surfed the web found material relevant to the lecture and added to their information; they also checked Facebook, email, and watched videos. The unplugged students performed significantly better on measures of memory and comprehension following the lecture. This proves that frequent interruptions scatter our thoughts and erode our memories.

Our lives have become crazy due to constant distractions. For instance, when I have to write a chapter, I move to a different part of the house from where my handheld devices live just so I can get through my day's quota of words. Lately, I have taken to escaping to Starbucks or the library. The constant ping of private messages and Facebook status updates are huge temptations when I am working on a piece of prose. I love my iPad and iPhone, but I don't appreciate how I can be reached anywhere anytime; I feel electronically stalked. When people email you, they expect an express response. Instant gratification has eroded our patience.

Everyone is rushing around to meet a deadline that is a constantly moving target. 'Time is money' is our modern-day mantra. We measure hours in dollars, not in sunrises and sunsets. There is no time to fritter away in useless pursuits like savouring a meal in slow bites or losing oneself in a much-loved melody. When was the last time you sat down and stared into space, simply letting your mind roam free?

Our fragmented attention does not enable us to fully tune into any one person or thing at a time. Mostly, we are not paying attention. When someone is talking to us, we are either staring at a device or rehearsing what we are going to say in response. The art of true listening is about being fully present, body and mind. We know whether we are listening to get a point across, argue someone out of the conversation, have the last word, win the word duel, or genuinely understand what the other thinks and feels about a subject. Is it surprising that we, often, have no memory of entire conversations or information exchanges that happened?

Frazzled and frantic, we have now begun to recognise that we need some way of dialling down, or we are going to be mentally wasted. People fork out hundreds of thousands of dollars to go to self-help seminars and learn mindfulness techniques. We are relearning how to breathe, smell, see, and listen to what is right in front of us instead of engaging with some virtual reality. We are learning how to drink a cup of tea, one sip at a time, not drink it down in absent-minded gulps.

Mahatma Gandhi once said that if we don't take just one step at a time, we end up tripping or hurting ourselves—or those around us. The Sufi mystic Meher Baba said, 'A mind that is fast is sick. A mind that is slow is sound. A mind that is still is divine.'

Dogs, babies, and toddlers are mindfulness gurus. Watch a dog go after a squirrel and you know there is nothing else in their world but that furry creature to be chased down.

It is a struggle to stay mindful in our noisy world. A practice that often helps me is the 'mindful pause'. About three to four times in a day, I remind myself to pause, close my eyes, and focus on my breath, slowing everything down. I tell myself that I don't have to get it all done *now*. At the end of my day, I celebrate small successes. If we don't bring a piece of peace and stillness into our days in a conscious, committed way, our brain will seize with overload.

Unfortunately, multitasking could well be Grace's reality moving forward. She is growing up in a world that consumes information in monstrous chunks at crazy speeds. But for now, Grace achieves every single milestone in her life at her own pace. We need to do the same as well. My little teacher is a master of focus. I am learning.

One Bite at a Time

1. Hold an apple in the palm of your hand and really look at it.
2. Bring it close to your nose and smell it.
3. Close your eyes and take a bite.
4. Feel the rush of juice fill your mouth.
5. Listen to the crunch as you chew.
6. Feel the texture of the fruit change shape and form.
7. You have just experienced an apple as fully and with as much presence as you can.

Chapter 16

I Have No Shame

Grace knows no shame because she is free from negative judgment. She runs around in her cute birthday suit, completely comfortable in her skin. She is, as yet, untouched by shame. I can't even begin to tell you how much it pains me to write those two words: as yet. For I know there will come a time in Grace's life when she will have to shake hands with shame, let it into her life, be bullied by it, and hide from it until she finds the awareness that lets her know that shame is the most universal human experience, one that brings with it many life lessons.

The most delightful no-shame story and memory I cherish of Grace is the time I taught her the location of her belly button. For some strange reason, she and her belly button became best buddies. She could not yet tell me where her nose was, but she caught on to the belly-button command in about thirty seconds and proudly lifted her shirt and showed off her navel when Mommy got home from work. This turned into an amusing game—she would lift her shirt up at regular intervals and inspect her belly button to make sure it was still there. We shared many laughs over it. But, then, Ms Smarty Pants soon figured that if she had a belly button, then, so must I. So, she proceeded to lift my shirt and check for mine. It was the best kind of belly-button bonding ever. It didn't matter who was around or where we were. Anytime she remembered the belly-button prompt, she would swiftly yank my shirt up and peer at mine.

***

Our parents made sure we behaved with the appropriate decorum. Far from being allowed to lift our shirts or pull down our underwear, we also learned to keep our elbows off the dining table, how to say please and thank you, and sit with our legs modestly crossed. But too early in our lives we learned that we must be ashamed of our bodies—too thin, too fat, too dark, too white, wrong shape, or wrong build. When we are ashamed of our bodies, we carry shame around like a contagious disease, because our body goes everywhere with us.

What is shame? Bestselling author, Brené Brown, who made it her life's work to study shame, says in her book, 'Shame is the intensely painful feeling or experience of believing that we are flawed and therefore unworthy of love and belonging.' It is the most primitive emotion we all feel and the one emotion no one wants to talk about. Brown also says that shame needs three things to thrive. If we put shame in a petri dish, add some secrecy, silence, and judgment, it grows exponentially. Put the same amount of shame in a petri dish and douse it with empathy, and you have created an environment that is hostile to shame. 'Shame depends on me buying into the belief that I'm alone,' Brown adds.[12]

Where does shame originate? Early in life, we internalise the messages we receive about ourselves from the adults in our lives, predominantly, our parents. If we were criticised, abused, wronged, humiliated, or, somehow, made to feel inadequate, we internalised those messages. We felt bad about it, and shame was born. If an adult we loved underscored that disapproval and verbalised it many times, we bottled up our shame, became defined and stunted by it. That is when we started to play small, settle for less, and shrank from life's stage.

Shame and guilt are often confused. The easiest way to differentiate the two is to understand that guilt says *I did something bad*, whereas shame says *I am bad*. Guilt is about the act, whereas shame is about feeling less than. Guilt has a redemptive aspect to it, while shame is corrosive, lethal, and damaging. When we focus on what we did wrong, we are able to correct it. When we believe that there is something inherently wrong with us, our basic sense of self is eroded.

Every one of us has something we are ashamed of. If it is not our bodies, it is how much we earn. If it is not our skin colour, it is our learning disability, inability to impress the opposite sex, or not being 'macho' enough to out-drink our buddies. Shame is like a huge ball we try and hold underwater, but the effort of keeping it there is tiring. So, when we let go, it bobs up to the surface and threatens us. And we indulge in different behaviours that we believe will keep shame at bay, some of which include embracing perfectionism, hanging out with the 'right crowd', and pretending to be someone we are not.

For myself, becoming more self-aware of where I experience shame has been a liberating experience. Other than carrying my father's alcoholic baggage, I also had shame around my gangly awkward physicality back in the day when I didn't know much about the right clothes, shoes, make-up, and so on. Getting a makeover that included a shoulder-length haircut made a world of difference to how I began to see myself. In my forties and fifties, embracing my worth as a divine being has helped soften the attachment to body image. I am a much more confident and self-assured woman; I am proud of my gifts and talents and compassionate towards my inadequacies.

Shame can be so damaging that an insensitive remark from an imperfect parent when we were six years old holds us captive and limits our potential well into our fifties.

When I was young, I was wrapped up in the shame of my father's alcoholism. None of my friends knew this truth about my family life—the discordant atmosphere and the disengaged behaviours. I never invited friends over to my house. What if my father staggered in through the front door piss-drunk? I never talked about my life at home. I felt like a sad victim and was often a jealous voyeur to others' lives and stories and experiences.

I vividly recall one specific incident. My father was travelling on business and slated to return home on a Thursday evening. We got an emotion-charged call from him that evening. He told us that his aircraft had made an emergency landing. The news was all over the media, and he was grateful to be coming home. He asked us to inform our neighbours with whom we enjoyed a close relationship. 'We must celebrate,' is how he ended the call before taking a taxi to get home. We fell for it hook, line, and sinker and invited our neighbours for a small celebratory gathering. But when we turned on the news, there was nothing about an averted air crash. About thirty minutes later, my father stumbled out of a taxi, wet and wobbly with alcohol. The air-crash story was nothing more than a figment of his hallucinatory imagination.

The neighbours greeted him awkwardly, excused themselves, and went home. My siblings, mother, and I felt soaked through with the shame of the situation. I wanted to die. Nothing less would kill the shame.

I was in my twenties when the lesson came to me, and it was Oprah Winfrey who released me from the captivity of my victim story as the child of an alcoholic. Sitting in my home in India and hearing Oprah say, 'Your truth can set someone else free' was life-changing. I truly believe that it opened me up in a way few things have. From that day, I made it a point to come right out and share my story. As I shared my story of shame, others began to open up and release their shame stories, too. Everyone has a shame story. If it isn't alcoholism, it is domestic abuse; if it isn't being poor, it is about never measuring up to a parent's gold standard.

That valuable lesson changed the trajectory of my life. I fully embraced the truth—vulnerability creates true connection. As soon as I opened my shame box and allowed people to look inside, they were equally willing to open their boxes, too. It was the most vital human connection I have experienced through telling a story I had kept hidden for far too long.

When we hold back and hide, we isolate.

In her bestselling book, Brown writes about the three things that we need to know about shame:

1. We all have it. Shame is universal and one of the most primitive human emotions that we experience. The only people who don't experience shame lack the capacity for empathy and human connection.
2. We're all afraid to talk about shame.
3. The less we talk about shame, the more control it has over our lives.[13]

Confessing is hard, but it is when I open my heart and tell a trusted friend the truth, my shame dissolves. Shame can only thrive in the dark. Bring it out into the light and it curls up and dies. Equally important to remember is that the person who hears your shame story must have earned your trust to do so.

Do men and women experience shame differently? Brown's work was mostly focused on women until a man walked up to her at a book signing and spoke the words that changed the way she saw shame and gender. 'We have shame,' he said to her. 'We have deep shame, but when we reach out and tell our stories, we get the emotional shit beat out of us.' This prompted Brown to study gender differences in shame. She discovered that appearance and body image are the number one shame triggers for women, whereas for men, it is the perception of weakness that triggers the maximum shame. '. . . show me a woman who can sit with a man in real vulnerability, in deep fear, and be with him in it, I will show you a woman who a) has done her work and b) does not derive her power from that man. And if you show me a man who can sit with a woman in deep struggle and vulnerability and not try to fix it, but just hear her and be with her and hold space for it, I'll show you a guy who's done his work . . . and doesn't derive his power from controlling and fixing everything.'[14]

According to Dr Linda Hartling, the director of Human Dignity and Humiliation Studies, a global and transdisciplinary network and fellowship of academics and practitioners, in order to deal with shame, some of us *move away* by withdrawing, hiding, silencing ourselves and keeping secrets. Some of us *move toward* by seeking to appease and please. And, some of us *move against* by trying to gain power over others, by being aggressive, and by using shame to fight shame (like sending really mean emails).[15]

When we have shame, we suffer from low self-esteem and do everything we can to pad our souls and stuff our intellects so that we can be enough. Wisdom traditions teach that self-love is the highest form of love. To love ourselves is our biggest challenge—to believe that our worthiness is not about how much we do, how much we own, or how much influence we possess. Shame is what we must overcome to understand and appreciate our inherent worthiness. It is a lesson we must learn all our lives—right till the very end when we may lose all control of who we are as a physical being and must lean on our loved ones even for activities of daily living. As a hospice volunteer, I have seen the end-of-life indignities that are visited upon people. Many need their bottoms wiped, catheters checked and reattached, or meals mashed and spoon-fed. It is a tough transition, especially, for those who prided themselves on their independence, fobbing off all attempts to give up their driver's license, move into a retirement home, and begin a life of slow dependence on others.

Grace's belly-button anecdote brings on a chuckle, but we all started life there—free of shame and judgment. I don't believe it is possible to steer clear of shame. Shame is part of our education. But we can choose not to be defined, limited, or cowed down by it. It is time to give ourselves a belly-button tickle and laugh about it, just like Grace does.

Reflection

1. Sit in silence and feel into your shame.
2. Go back to the place and time where your shame originated.
3. What messages did you receive that anchored the shame?
4. Grab pen and paper and make two columns. In the first column, write down your shame statements. In the second, write what a loving being would say about what you experience as shameful.
5. Revisit the loving statements and read them until they begin to trickle into your consciousness.

Chapter 17

I Have Enough

As soon as Grace mastered the art of using her hands to feed herself little treats, she learned that it was fun to share. She would grab a fistful of strawberry puffs or little crunchers and hold them out for me. As her motor skills improved, she figured that feeding me was an even better idea. So, every time she ate something, she had to feed me, too.

Not once did she peek into her snack catcher to see how many puffs she had left or check to make sure she had enough before she stuffed them in my mouth. I laughed at her efforts, and she laughed when I laughed.

Sharing is one of the earliest lessons we learn in childhood—share your toys; share your candy; share your crayons.

Once the ego-self starts to take shape, the concepts of 'mine' and 'yours' take root. That is when toddlers become attached to their possessions and wail painfully when a visiting cousin grabs a toy from them. To make sure that kids have great in-home training, parents decide to get pregnant a second time. Siblings are great for sharing practice.

Unfortunately, the lesson changes shape and form as we grow older, and we morph into varying degrees of

Scrooge from *A Christmas Carol*. The mentality of lack infects us, and we begin to hoard, lest we run out. The word 'hoard' may seem a little extreme here, but if we were honest, the tendency to stockpile manifests in our lives in one way or another. I am a self-confessed book hoarder. Why is it better than hoarding shoes or cat food or paper towels? I don't know! It probably doesn't seem as pathological, but it is the same attachment that lives at the root of it—I resist giving my books away.

We have all witnessed examples of this phenomenon when the weather channel warns us of an impending blizzard. We run out to the nearest grocery store and buy more-than-we-need quantities of milk, bread, toilet paper, cereal, fruit, and other supplies, just so we are barricaded and safe if nature decides to throw our lives into complete disarray.

Unfortunately, this hoarding mentality lasts well beyond nature's storms. Life's storms rage inside our fearful heads, so we live our lives believing we will never have enough. Living in the space of lack can be a source of great stress. The 2008 economic recession also added energy to the epidemic of paranoia. We are constantly in fight-or-flight mode about jobs, home mortgages, college tuitions, and the like.

'Lack' and 'abundance' are states of mind, not the size of bank accounts.

Spiritual teacher and bestselling author, Wayne W. Dyer, says, 'Abundance is not something we acquire. It is something we tune into.' This definition speaks to the power of vibration, the invisible energy we emit which other people feel. So, if we emanate the vibration of love and compassion and joy, that is the frequency we will draw into our life experiences. People, opportunities, and situations that are vibrating on the same frequency will flow into our life.

Our belief creates our reality. If we approach the world with an abundance consciousness, the Universe will open doors to more abundance for us. Conversely, if we view the world through the lens of scarcity, lack and limitation become our reality.

There are many inspiring examples of ordinary folks with extraordinary dreams who have achieved immense wealth and success. These people didn't start out with any money worth speaking about! Howard Schultz, CEO of Starbucks, shared in a recent interview that he didn't have a dime, but he had a powerful dream. Two hundred investors turned him down, but he picked himself up each time, fuelled by the force within that believed. This theme is common to most success stories; their currency was self-belief.

Wealth is usually manifested through the power of thought. If these people had focused on *I don't have . . .* or *I'll never . . .* or *I cannot . . .* we wouldn't be drinking Starbucks coffee or using iPhones or flying Virgin Atlantic.

I agree it is hard to ignore the knot in our gut when the mortgage bill drops into the mailbox. Fear is part of the human condition. Yet, collaborating with fear instead of fighting it works best. Fear as fuel motivates us to take action. Fear as paralysis keeps us frozen and stuck.

Wisdom teacher and author of the bestselling *Conversations with God* series, Neale Donald Walsch, asks the question: 'How do we tell ourselves that we have enough when the reality is a single dollar bill in our wallet? Well, if that person sees himself as richer than the guy with ten cents in his pocket.'

The Laws of the Universe never fail. We need little convincing when it comes to the law of gravity because it affects everything we do, but we remain ignorant of the other laws. The Law of Giving states that: '. . . giving and receiving are different aspects of the flow of energy in the universe. And in our willingness to give that which we seek, we keep the abundance of the universe circulating in our lives.'[16]

All the wisdom traditions teach that the easiest way to get what you want is to help another find the same thing—whether it is love, money, time, patience, friendship, understanding, or acceptance.

Do I have all the money to feel safe and secure into my old age? No. Do I have enough for where I am right now and what I need? Yes. Do I feel rich? Absolutely!

To me, good health is abundance.

Great friendships are abundance.

A loving, connected family is abundance.

The opportunity to make a difference in the world is abundance.

If I had a million bucks and none of the above, would that make me rich? The answer is an unequivocal no.

Grace reminds me that it is in the sharing of simple things that true abundance lives. In a shared cheese puff is a world of pure joy and togetherness. She has enough . . . and more. And I need to remember, so do I.

Experience Abundance

When you are feeling down and out and experiencing lack, whether it is in the area of money, relationships, health, or fulfilling work, do this simple exercise. Start from the letter A and go all the way to Z, making a list of things you have in your life.

For instance, your list can include Amazing friends, Books, Clean drinking water, etc.

The very act of writing this list moves your vibration from lack to sufficiency, or even better, abundance.

Every time you are tempted to complain about what you don't have, get a sheet of paper and start making this list.

Chapter 18

I HOLD NO GRUDGES

A baby has enough reasons to be peeved at adults. Grace certainly had her share of Uma-peeves. The time when she wanted a sip of my coffee, and I said a firm no; when she fought an afternoon nap, and I asserted that she needed to rest for a while; when I insisted that the poopy diaper she wanted to hang on to belonged in the diaper pail. I can recall many occasions when she has kicked and wailed in protest, trying to push a boundary. Even though she was unable to articulate it, I am pretty sure this is what she would have said if she could: 'I don't like it when you say no; I don't like that you are bigger and stronger and able to strap that diaper on my butt; I don't like that you are so tall and can place that beautiful china doll up and out of my reach.'

Yet, babies don't hold grudges. If they did, adults would be in big trouble. God knows we mess up often enough. But babies have no concept of past and future, they are simply grounded in the present moment. It is this amazing intuitive gift that helps them not hold onto grudges. Everything that happened five minutes ago simply evaporates.

When Grace was disgruntled because I had turned down a request, the neighbourhood lawnmowers always came to my rescue. I would whisk her off to one of the living room windows every time a lawn mower was in action. Something about the dull roar of that machine as it smoothed out a beautiful emerald-green lawn would calm her down instantly, my misdemeanour of a moment ago, forgotten. Nose pressed to the windowpane, she would move her head, following the direction of the lawnmower. All was forgotten, and we were best buddies again.

Why do adults hold onto stuff that happened thirty or forty years ago? We hold fast to thoughts and opinions about what happened a long time ago, and we bring them to bear on how we see the situation and the offender today. We were wounded by imperfect parents (and Grace, I am sure, will have her share of scars), and those wounds become stories with triggers if not attended to. It is the narrative we carry about what happened which is the source of most of our emotional pain.

I ended a friendship that meant a lot to me because of the power of the story I was telling myself about the situation. Nan and I had a friendship going back to our high-school years. In our thirties and busy raising kids and balancing the needs of a household, we still carved out time to drink coffee and chat about our lives. She was going through some marital struggles and would call me often in the middle of a stressed situation. I made it a point to always listen and offer counsel. One evening, she called me in tears about the latest drama playing out in her life. I listened patiently for fifteen minutes, and said, 'Nan, it's my birthday, and I'm getting ready to go out to dinner.' Flustered that she had forgotten my birthday, she issued a flurry of apologies and hung up. And that is when my storytelling brain went into overdrive.

She doesn't care about me or my life.

All she wants is a good listener and she has one in me.

She is selfish and never calls me except when she has to rant.

Wounded and angry, I cut myself off from Nan's life. It was more than a year later when my mother was diagnosed with cancer and my perspective on life changed that I reconnected with her, apologised, and made amends. She clarified that she loved me and always had. I recognised that she did care; she was just not very good about remembering birthdays and anniversaries.

Today, I understand that I need to accept people where they are. People only hurt us if we allow them to. In other words, how I choose to interpret what happens and how well I define my boundaries go a long way in how people treat me.

Babies don't take things personally and make it about them. The foot-stomping toddler is simply a two-year-old wanting their own way and expressing a growing sense of self.

Some days, when my husband walks in the door after a twelve-hour workday, our expectations clearly don't intersect. He is dialling down and needs downtime, and I am ready for connection. I have to be really watchful about how I interpret his need for silence. If I am not careful, I start to make up stories that he is rarely interested in my day, or that I always come last in his life. Then, there are days when I am calm and able to shrug off his monosyllabic grunts as just a bad-day-at-the-workplace.

Aside from intimate relationships which can be a minefield to navigate some days, all of us have had experiences in the real world that challenge us. It could be the driver who cuts into our lane or the sullen checkout clerk who ticks us off. Instead of offering generous understanding, we judge and vent and curse.

With every transgression—major or minor—there is an opportunity for understanding, even forgiveness. Often, we fail to address these forgiveness issues, so they keep piling up until they are so huge that they bury us. That is when we turn inwards and begin to hate who we are, but the true self in us knows that we are inherently good and so is everyone else. If only we could learn from babies, we would forgive, let go, and be happy.

Spiritual teacher and bestselling author, Eckhart Tolle, tells a story in his book where he observes how ducks fight. After two ducks get into a fight, they separate and float off in different directions. Then, each duck flaps its wings vigorously, shaking off the surplus energy built up during the fight. The fight is over. Life moves on.

Tolle says: 'If the duck had a human mind, it would keep the fight alive by thinking, by story-making. The duck's story would probably go like this: "I don't believe what he just did. He came to within five inches of me . . . He thinks he owns this pond. I'll never trust him again. I'm sure he's plotting something already. But I'm not going to stand for this. I'll teach him a lesson he won't forget."'[17]

On and on the mind spins its tales, thinking and talking about it days, months, or years later. The fight continues, and the body generates emotion in response to the energy of those still-active thoughts. Emotions create more thoughts and the cycle continues. You can see how problematic the duck's life would become if it had a human mind. But this is how most humans live all the time. No situation or event is ever really finished. The mind and the mind-made 'me and my story' keep it going.

I have a favourite Zen story, one that illustrates the same truth. Two monks were walking along a muddy, slushy road following heavy rains when they came upon a young woman who was struggling to cross the road. One of the monks picked her up and carried her to the other side. The woman went off and the monks continued their journey, walking in silence. Five hours later, one monk said to the other, 'Why did you carry the girl across the road? We are monks. You know we are not supposed to touch women.' The second monk replied, 'I put her down hours ago. Why are you still carrying her?'

It is our unwillingness to let go that causes problems. Forgiveness is tricky, but life can never be fully lived if we don't learn how to forgive. All the accumulated resentment, anger, hatred, and hurt cause us more pain than our offender.

We also don't know how to do this work and, often, are attached to outcomes. How do I forgive? How do I ask for forgiveness? What if he doesn't accept my apology? What if she thinks I am weak? Will I be violated again? Letter or verbal apology? Email or face-to-face? We get entangled in a variety of questions. Mired in these million dilemmas, often, forgiveness is the casualty.

Forgiveness, like love, is a choice. It is a gift we give ourselves. It is the one and only path to peaceful living. Often misunderstood as weakness, forgiveness, in reality, is about courage. It is not about letting the offender off the hook, it is about letting go of our pain and suffering. It frees us from the chains of the past.

Spiritually evolved teachers tell us that, in the ultimate reality, there is nothing to forgive because there was nothing wrong in the first place. Everything that happens, happens in utter divine perfection between souls who co-create the experience for learning, growth, and evolution. It's like a play where the actors sign a contract to take on certain roles and speak, act, and behave in ways that make the characters come alive, affect the storyline and advance the plot. Viewed from that perspective, we are simply helping each other grow through the choices we make.

Forgiveness is divine, as Grace, a pure child of Spirit, teaches me over and over. That is how she is able to thrive in the space of unsullied joy, unencumbered by life's tally of rights and wrongs. It is also the only way for us as adults to experience the peace that passes all understanding.

Untangling the Knot

1. Sit down in a comfortable place and close your eyes.
2. Take a few deep centring breaths.
3. Bring to mind a person whom you have trouble forgiving.
4. Imagine a cord running from your navel to the navel of this person that connects you through this hurtful act. It is a cord that tugs and binds you to the other.

5. Now, visualise a powerful white light surround this cord, and watch the cord dissolve and melt away.
6. In your own words, say a prayer of release. It could be something like: 'I now free you so that I can live in peace. We are no longer bound by this hurtful act.'
7. Breathe in peace and breathe out forgiveness.

Chapter 19

I Have Everything I Need
for My Journey

In the twenty months that Grace has been here, I can't ever remember a time when she suffered any anxiety about her human journey. How could she? She has no prior life experience to frame her expectations. What she does have is an instinct to obey universal law, the divine energy that shapes every moment of her life.

Babies don't toss and turn in their cribs, fretting about why they just cannot seem to master walking from the living room to the kitchen without landing on their butt half a dozen times. They don't worry whether Mom loves them anymore because of how irritable she was at the sticky mess made at mealtime. They rarely obsess over whether they will grow hair, teeth, or nails when all their cousins of approximately the same age seem to be enjoying accelerated results.

Babies trust the divine perfection and order in the Universe. So did we when we were little until society cured us of it. Babies live and grow from pure instinct—they are totally heart-centred beings because the part of their brain that will come to perform logical and rational functions in the world is still developing. It is a scientific fact that the first heart cell beats as early as only four weeks after conception. The heart is, in fact, the first organ of human development—it begins to form much before the brain.

If you think about it, everything that emanates from divine origination trusts that it has everything for its journey here. All except man. We come into this earthly experience fully formed and trusting in the goodness of it all. Then, we grow up and our mind takes over. As it starts to chatter, we don't like who we are, and we are paranoid that we will never be rich or happy, find someone who will love us, or make a living doing what we are passionate about.

The oak doesn't ever want to be a rose bush. Nor does the humble acorn fret and fume when it looks skyward at all the mighty oaks and wonder just how much longer it will have to wait to enjoy the same view. The magic and mystery of divinity is that the minuscule acorn contains everything it needs to grow into a towering oak. And the beauty of it all is that the acorn never doubts it for a moment because it doesn't have a mind to ruin its journey to greatness.

If only we would trust in the wisdom that fused a sperm and egg at the perfect moment in eternity to produce you and me. If only we could stop doubting and know in the deepest part of our being that the source that shaped our nose has the shape of our life figured out, too.

Our need to control our journey is what causes us to drive into life's dead ends. We mistakenly believe that we have the power to manoeuvre outcomes to suit our exact preferences, so we grasp and cling and control. The truth is, we don't have to strive to move any of the pieces of life, we just need to ask for the guidance to know the right moves to make at the right time. Life lived like that can be a joyous experience.

What gets in the way and trips us up is our belief in the illusion that somewhere out there are all our answers. Yet, one of the most fundamental truths I am constantly being reminded of is what Martha Graham, modern dancer and choreographer, said to her dear friend Agnes de Mille, also a celebrated choreographer. Graham said: 'There is a vitality, a life force, an energy, a quickening that is translated through you into action, and because there is only one of you in all time, this expression is unique. And if you block it, it will never exist through any other medium and it will be lost. The world will not have it. It is not your business to determine how good it is nor how valuable nor how it compares with other expressions. It is your business to keep it yours, clearly and directly, to keep the channel open. . . .'

The essence of who I am and who you are is unique. Your journey is yours, mine is mine. It follows, therefore, that all the wisdom you need for that journey can only be within you. I hold my map. No one else can. If I look to you for my answers, I am immediately off course. This is one of the most liberating truths I have come to realise on my earthly journey.

You and I are like brilliant computers programmed with all the software upgrades we need to live our lives on purpose and experience joy and fulfilment. The problem is that what we remembered as children, we have forgotten as adults. We look to the external markers of success and convince ourselves that we are lacking in some way, doing something wrong, that success and meaning are the privilege of a chosen few.

When I was new to the spiritual work I do now—
trying to teach workshops and finding opportunities
to speak—I was scheduled to give a talk at one of the
libraries in my area. Excited, I had prepared a bunch
of solid notes for my session. I walked into the library
and felt my heart quicken when I spied a poster with
my name and the title of my talk. I stepped into the
appointed room and wrote down the title of my talk
on the whiteboard with a bold flourish. A few minutes
went by, but no one walked through the door. Twenty
minutes later, still no one. A half hour went by, and,
then, a full forty-five minutes. Not one single person
walked through that door. My optimism slowly began to
crumble, and I had to face the truth: no one was going
to show up. Nobody cared. Eyes misting, I gathered my
notes and, somehow, managed to walk out of the library
holding it together. As soon as I got into my car, my
fragile emotions spilled out. Forehead against the cold
steering wheel, I sobbed my heart out. I begged, pleaded,
and yelled at God. My rant went something like this:

> *If this is what you want me to be doing, why didn't
> you send people my way? I worked so hard for
> this evening. I prepared. I researched. I had some
> great wisdom to share. But I guess this is all just a
> pipe dream. You don't really want me to succeed.
> Because you did nothing, absolutely nothing to
> help. I thought you were my partner. I'm not doing
> this anymore. I give up.*

It was the perfect moment for me to experience my
smallness and convince myself that I was never going
to make it teaching what I loved, what my heart longed

to share, and what I knew I was born to do. I compared myself with every coach and speaker whose reality was sold-out events and success in bold letters.

This is typically what we do. We compare the worst of ourselves with the best of others. We look at someone's current chapter and judge the story of their entire life based on that single chapter without pausing to consider that, maybe, they had a terrible chapter two months ago. Theodore Roosevelt knew what he was talking about when he said, 'Comparison is the thief of joy.'

I have since come to realise the truth that what's in the way is the way. If someone had told me in that moment of despair that just a few years later I would enjoy the kind of success I believed was reserved for the chosen few, I would have laughed in their face. As it turned out, two of my 2016 events in southern India were huge successes. My workshop on forgiveness was so overbooked that the organisers had to change the venue to accommodate the extra attendees. And a couple of days after that, close to a hundred women signed up for my one-hour talk on 'What Loss Teaches Us'.

I am the only one who has my map. And it is up to me to figure out what my path looks like and how I will travel it.

Rarely do we pause to listen to the voice within that will gently lead us home. But a gift arrived in my life in the form of deep soul writing taught by a cherished teacher, Janet Conner. Soul writing is one of my favourite ways to connect with my inner wisdom. My daily meditation practice is another. When I get quiet and ask, I receive exactly what I need—even if I don't always agree with what my Maker sends me. Confusion melts away and clarity emerges. My inner wisdom knows what is good for me, even when I don't. The books I am guided to write, the opportunities I am guided to follow, the people I am guided to contact—one magical door leads to another.

When I forget to listen and my ego begins to assert itself, I experience struggle and frustration. It is a sign that I have wandered off into the wilderness, distracted by the noises of the world, following some bright shiny object and its trail of lure.

Watching Grace just 'be' joy is a beautiful lesson in self-containment. For now, she is secure in who she is and where she needs to go, just happy to let the magical journey unfold, one milestone at a time. No rush. No struggle. No comparisons.

At twenty months, she speaks a handful of words, but she never doubts that there is a world of words inside of her, just waiting to tumble out in the divine perfection of time.

Letter to Your Young Self

1. Get a sheet of paper and sit yourself down in a quiet space.
2. Close your eyes and centre your awareness on your breath.
3. Bring to mind an image of yourself at a time in your life when you felt lost and confused.
4. Look him/her in the eye and see your soul.
5. With where you are right now, see yourself speaking to your young self and telling him/

her what you wished you knew at that age.

6. When you are done, open your eyes and write down that wisdom in the form of a letter addressed to your young self.

7. When you feel buffeted by the winds of change or confusion, read this letter and bring to mind your innate wisdom.

Chapter 20

I Trust

Every time Grace cried, she trusted me to take care of her discomfort. Sometimes, it was a soggy diaper, other times, an annoying tooth pushing its way up her tender gum. Or the law of gravity doing its thing as she clambered onto the couch.

As she grew older, she trusted her dad to hold on tight and not let go as he swung her upside down, and she squealed with pure joy, wanting more. She trusted her mom would come home and cuddle with her every evening. She trusted that I would hold her for as long as she wanted me to when she needed comfort.

All babies are born with a biological preparedness to trust. They come into the world with a clean trust scale, almost knowing how to trust instinctively. They trust in their potential to grow and become more of who they are, never questioning, wondering, or doubting. A baby never has to think or say, 'My intention is to grow into an adult.' Just as an acorn doesn't ever have to intend to grow into an oak tree. All that a child needs for their development is in-built at the factory. Nurture provides the rest. It is no different for the acorn. A mighty oak sleeps inside that tiny seed, ready to awaken to its fullest potential, provided all the right conditions for growth are met.

But stories of extreme neglect are equally true. Babies in baskets abandoned on church doorsteps. Babies who are denied basic survival needs, and babies who are killed because they were born with a vagina, not a penis.

Even babies raised in the most loving homes must deal with some degree of broken trust.

As we grow older, that tender five-letter word is shattered over and over again. In my case, it was my alcoholic father's broken promises. He never came home when he said he would. Never took me to the park when he said he would. Never came to my school plays when he said he would. 'Never' is a big word in a little child's heart.

One broken agreement on top of another, and, soon, there was a tall pile. I used every one of them to build walls around me—tall and sturdy enough so no one could see me and, more important, break me any further than I already was.

It took years of learning and self-discovery to start chipping away at those walls. It took the love of my gentle *Amma* and the blessings of a forgiving grandma. It took the kind brown eyes of a freckle-faced nun in college who introduced me to God.

We are all broken and boarded up as adults. It is our way of surviving in a world that slights us, knowingly and unknowingly, in many ways. We make the walls impenetrable and wallpaper them with acceptable language such as 'cool', 'I don't care', and 'whatever'. It is a way of verbally fending off potential threats. Vulnerability is as loaded a word as a gun put to the head. No one wants to go there.

Suspicion and cynicism, we believe, will keep us safe from the slingshots of insensitivity.

There is a flip side to the whole trust issue. What we believe is safety, is often shutdown. When we are unwilling to trust, we close off our hearts to our fellow humans. We disempower the value of connection. Our friendships begin to have severe boundaries, and we are fenced off from each other. Others read our 'Do Not Enter' sign well before they reach us. Most times, they are wearing variations of the sign, too. And so, one mask meets another and what could have been an intimate encounter is, often, just an artificial, flavoured version of the real thing.

When we dig deeper, we realise that failure to trust the other is, about failure to trust ourselves. A memorable *Dr. Phil* (an American talk show) moment comes to mind. Dr Phil, a popular talk show host, author, and social commentator, was doing a segment on marital affairs. A woman spoke about how her husband had cheated on her by having an affair with her best friend. She was caught in the dilemma of whether to forgive him and take him back or not. She confessed that she didn't know if she could trust him again. What Dr Phil said in response has stayed with me all these years: 'The question is, can you trust yourself?' If she trusted herself, she would know exactly what to do if her husband repeated the offense. She would be safe because she would trust in her own decisions and choose what was best for her.

How is self-trust broken? When we make agreements and don't keep them, we stop trusting ourselves. If we agree to meet a friend for dinner or promise to accompany our mother-in-law to the beauty salon, we would think a hundred times before breaking that agreement, no matter how tempted we are to do something different. We don't like letting others down, but we have little trouble letting ourselves down.

Self-trust erodes very quickly, with every broken agreement—when we promised to workout three times a week and simply drove past the gym; when we committed to writing ten pages and goofed off on social media; when we swore we would stop stuffing our sadness but did it again; and instead of calling a friend, we copped out and devoured a four-cheese pizza in the company of a flat-screen television and an indifferent cat.

Each time this happens, the little voice in the head gets an ammo amp: 'Told you, you're nothing but a loser! Never keep your word, do ya?'

When we can barely keep our contracts with ourselves, how can we trust others to keep their contracts with us?

Soon, the I-don't-trust-me and I-don't-trust-you voices blend. They join hands and begin to have fun. The question is: how do we learn to trust? What is the guarantee that people will do what they say they will? For me, the answer lies in the word 'compassion'.

I have made agreements with people that I haven't delivered on. So, when someone does that to me, I try and remind myself that I have been there, done that. I reach inside myself to find that place of compassion for others.

Over time, I have learned to fess up when I mess up. Taking ownership for my broken agreements is the best way for me to align with my integrity. I realise that if I keep breaking agreements and resist taking responsibility, I create a reputation as an 'agreement-breaker'.

The same is true for others. So, I need to define boundaries. I am willing to overlook a couple of broken agreements. Compassion must not be confused with tolerance. If the person keeps reneging on promises, I must cut my losses and move on.

We teach people how to treat us. What does this look like?

If I have committed to meeting someone at noon and am running late by fifteen minutes, I can either text or call to inform them. But if I repeat this behaviour three times, I would only have myself to blame for the 'Late Kate' reputation I earn.

If someone promised to email me a piece of information on a particular day but was unable to, an email from them (ahead of the promised deadline) requesting more time would show me they cared. Then again, if this became a pattern, my trust in their ability to deliver to a deadline would certainly be broken.

But how do we keep our hearts open when our trust has been broken repeatedly? By engaging in dialogue and trying to understand the other's perspective before jumping to judgment.

Let's face it. We are the walking wounded. We all have trust issues because of the imperfections visited on us by the authority figures from our childhood. The challenge is to recognise where those wounds are and learn from them. Shut down or heart-centred? We get to make this choice in every situation.

Just as Grace will. As her experience with the word 'trust' shifts and changes with the people who walk through her world, she will come a full circle with trust. As we all must. That is the only way we can stay open to life's magic and joy.

The Next Best Step

1. Bring to mind a problem you are struggling with and seeking a solution to.
2. Take a few moments to sit still, relax, and breathe.
3. Place a hand on your heart and ask: 'What is the next best step for me to take?'
4. Trust whatever comes up—a word, an image, a song, an idea, or, even, nothing. Maybe, right now is time for no action.
5. In the next week or two, pay attention to how you feel about what you have received. Build your trust muscle by checking in with your own wisdom.

Chapter 21

I FEEL MY FEELINGS

When I walk in the door to visit with Grace, joy lights up her eyes, her face, her entire being. When her request for a Barney video is turned down, she cries tears of sadness. When she tries to slowly crawl her way down the stairs to the basement and Mama grabs her with a firm no, she kicks her chubby legs and is royally mad. When monsters sneak into her dreams at night, she startles awake and screams until a parent shows up to soothe her back to sleep. A variety of emotions sweep through Grace.

Crying, stomping, joyfully jiggling one's butt—it is all good when you are a child. Children have no judgments about their feelings; they feel what they feel and allow the feelings to flow out of their bodies.

Children also learn very early what is okay to feel and what is not. If a parent expects them to cover up their sadness and present a brave front to the world, that is what they do.

My parents didn't get a lot of things right, but they gave me a great gift. I was really fortunate to grow up in a home where tears were understood and validated. When one of my siblings or I cried, everyone rallied around, lent a shoulder and a listening ear. We hugged and kissed a lot. Emotional expression was totally accepted.

For many people, that is not the case. The earliest authority figures in their lives were not always the best models of emotional expression. Growing up, they may have received messages that didn't give them permission to feel. Some of the most common responses modelled for us in early childhood were: 'Suck it up and soldier on' or 'Boys don't cry' or 'Don't let your face show what your heart feels' or 'If you pretend it isn't happening, it won't.'

So, we have become really good at stuffing our sorrow, redirecting our rage, hiding our hurts, and tucking away our tears. We take on our family's emotional legacy and set it as our default mode. Over time, the message was reinforced. The better you are at hiding your emotions, the stronger you are.

Unmet needs don't simply disappear. The four-year-old who experienced rejection still craves acceptance. The six-year-old who could never do anything right in her/his dad's eyes becomes the person who constantly seeks accolades from his bosses and peers. We go through life looking for people who will give us what our parents and siblings were unable to. If we haven't attended to our inner child's needs, the needs that were thwarted when we were three, or five, or eight, chances are, a four-year-old is running our forty-year-old life.

In his book, *Whatever Arises, Love That: A Love Revolution That Begins with You*, author Matt Kahn says, 'No matter how daunting, overwhelming, or uncomfortable your experiences seem to be, the ups and downs of everyday life can be transformed into a deeply fulfilling spiritual adventure, simply by becoming the source of your own fulfilment. . . . This is why loving what arises is the single most important way to fulfil your divine destiny. . . . By acknowledging the deeper healing that occurs when allowing each emotion to be openly felt, you have already taken your first exciting step toward loving what arises.'[18]

Karla McLaren, a scientist who has devoted her life to studying, writing, and teaching about emotions, says that we experience a total of seventeen negative emotions and only three positive emotions—joy, contentment, and happiness. No wonder we feel blue more often about everything in life. This tells us that we need to make a conscious effort to stay positive. However, those who look to the self-help industry for answers, sometimes, embrace the notion that to be more spiritual or positive, they must bypass what is negative. But the truth is—you cannot leap over what is uncomfortable by writing affirmations or keeping a gratitude journal.

Feelings that we push away—anger, fear, and sadness—serve a real purpose. Anger lets us know that a boundary has been crossed; fear alerts us to take protective action; grief asks the question: what must be released? If we are not paying attention to our emotional messengers, we are not responding to life in its totality.

We have not grown up with permission to express what we feel. And we are expected, for the most part, to put a lid on our emotions at the workplace. Unsure and confused about emotional expression, we enter the realm of intimate relationships in our twenties. We feel heard and loved during the heady days of romance, but when it is time to move into the commitment phase, all our fears rise to the surface. We bump up against our partner's emotional history. All of a sudden, there is emotional warfare. He doesn't understand why you have to be so 'sensitive' and cry about everything. She is bewildered that he just locks up his emotions, tosses the key, and walks away. I am willing to bet that garbled emotion-speak has caused more harm in human relationships than anything else.

So, then, we take our significant other, a credit card, and a bag full of emotional woes to a therapist with impressive degrees. And where do they take you? Right back to your childhood, the origin of all dysfunctions. It really is a full-circle moment.

Stuffed feelings don't simply evaporate. Traditional Chinese medicine, which has been practiced for over five thousand years, associates five major organ systems with particular emotions. It says that the liver and gall bladder are associated with anger, the heart and small intestine with joy, the spleen and stomach with overthinking, the lungs and large intestine with grief, and the kidneys and bladder with fear. Emotions live in our hips and gut and back, in our kidneys and liver and nerves. In some cases, ignored and abandoned emotions turn into terminal illnesses and autoimmune disorders. There is a wonderfully wise saying: 'Tears that are not shed make other organs weep.' Irrespective of the messages we received during childhood, increased self-awareness in adulthood can help us make choices that serve our well-being. It is a good idea to choose being in touch with our feelings as a way to a healthier life—mentally, spiritually, and physically.

Emotions simply want to move through us. Energy + Motion = Emotion. If we pound a pillow, we allow anger to move through and out of us. When we sob, we allow sadness a safe exit from our body. Once the energy has moved out, it changes form, and we are no longer stewing in toxins that endanger our well-being.

But the judgments we carry about emotions halt us. Weak, out-of-control, impulsive, dramatic, messy. *Slap! Slap! Slap!* Out come the labels, and for fear of incurring others' disapproval, we hide, pretend, and deny our feelings.

The Buddhists teach us to befriend our feelings, to move towards them with curiosity instead of turning away in fear. Why do we resist enquiry? How would it feel if, instead of defending a point of view out of fear, we got quiet and asked ourselves, 'What about this situation makes me afraid and want to attack the other? What layer do I need to peel away to find what is buried beneath it?'

We don't have an emotional map or a vocabulary we can turn to, so stepping into the territory of emotions, often, feels like blundering in the darkness. A great first step would be to get curious. It is useful to ask: 'Why am I feeling this?' instead of catapulting to: 'He makes me feel so . . .' which is our default blame-and-shame game. This grows our soul.

Softening the heart is a practice. When we soften our heart, we completely accept every emotion that arises. There is no judgment or displeasure. Emotions aren't good or bad, they just are. They have been given to us to be used as a reliable compass. When something produces joy and makes your heart sing, it is your Spirit going, 'Yes! Yes! That's what you are here to do.' And when you get that roiling oily feeling in your gut that screams, 'Stay away from that person or situation or side street!' it is intuition protecting you, steering you out of harm's way.

Research tells us that the tears that leak from our eyes when we chop onions are very different from the tears we produce when we are crying from grief. The chemical composition of the latter includes stress hormones and toxins, a testimony to the body's wisdom. We are meant to use that safety valve to release the tension from our bodies, not lock them up for an illusory badge of 'Braveheart'.[19]

Christina Rasmussen, author of *Second Firsts: Live, Laugh and Love Again,* says that she couldn't cry for almost three months after losing her thirty-five-year-old husband to cancer. And, then, one day, she tripped and fell at home. That little accident set her off. She couldn't stop sobbing for hours, not because she was in physical distress, but because her body finally had permission to release the river of tears she had been holding inside.

The next time you feel a prickly sensation at the back of your throat and a sting in your eyes, give yourself the gift of an ugly cry. If you fear judgment, take yourself to the bathroom. But get those toxins out of you.

In the span of five minutes, Grace can cry, laugh, stomp her feet, and be mad. But then she is centred. There are no hidden emotional closets inside her. Let us take a leaf out of her book and focus on improving our emotional quotient.

Soft Belly Breathing

1. Settle down in a comfortable position and close your eyes.
2. Bring to mind an event that triggers a specific emotion: anger, fear, or sadness.
3. Bring your attention to your belly.

4. Breathe into your belly and feel it soften.
5. Breathe out and be with the emotion.
6. Repeat this breathing pattern for five minutes.
7. You will notice how breathing, softening, and allowing creates an openness in your heart. It opens the door to let in everything with no judgment. From this space, clarity and compassion arise.

Chapter 22

I Know Who I Am

I watched with pride and joy as Grace learned to attach names and words to people and things. When she didn't have the language for doll versus ball, or milk versus juice, she would point towards what she wanted and say 'mmm mmm' while she waited for me to figure it out. But, gradually, she learned to say shoe, bird, fish, apple, and so much more. Given her growing word-a-minute vocabulary, a new list of words was already outdated on my next visit with her.

Grace and I had a rich, wholesome language even before words entered the picture. Eye contact, smiles, and gurgles spoke volumes while she waited for words to emerge. There was a sacredness to our silent communication.

In her two's, Grace began to navigate her world using the map of language and began to develop labelling skills. She even had a language of her own which was as original as her fingerprints. My favourite Gracie words are *guck* (stuck), *two* (to indicate she wants more of something whether it is gumdrops, hugs, or being swung or twirled), *ee-ee* (monkey), *godurt* (yogurt), and *wawa* (water).

Around the time I became Grace's nanny, I had started to deepen my spiritual quest. I had begun to get curious about energy versus matter. Everything in the world—from tables, laptops, cars and chairs to people, animals, flowers, and bugs—is energy. Things are more than just things. We are more than just a cluster of labels: a name, occupation, and role. Clearly, I had started out as a single cell, but where did I come from? And where would I return to when this earthly journey was over? I became increasingly obsessed with a primal question: who am I?

For many years prior, my identity had been inextricably intertwined with my 'wife' self, my 'Mum' self, or my 'writer' self—depending upon the role I was starring in during that particular phase of my life. It was easy to fall in love with the idea of being married, so I slipped into being Mrs Girish. My new last name rolled off my tongue easily and made me feel extra special, like I had graduated to one of life's most important milestones. I slipped into being a 'stay-at-home mum' with equal felicity. When I started to wear my 'writer' hat, my sense of self became invested in every published article and short story that won an award. As a 'corporate trainer', I soaked up the appreciation that came my way from gratified students. In short, it was easy to give myself over to the ego agendas the roles served.

When my mother passed away in 2009, all those roles crumbled around me. Motherless and unanchored, I was adrift in a sea of confusion. Somehow, my mother had always been the family sun, and we, the loyal satellites, knew our place and roles around her. When she died, a thunderbolt hit me in the form of 'Who *really* am I now?' All those I ams that I had been saying all my life: 'I am Uma', 'I am Ruki's mum', 'I am Hindu', 'I am from India', and 'I am a writer' are all part of my human, physical reality. Yet, a voice from within whispered, 'You are more, much more.' I am more than my limiting labels. A personality cannot contain the whole spirit.

Thus, began a journey of seeking and exploration. Spiritually enlightening seminars, mentors, soul journaling and searching brought glimmers of clarity. I knew it in my heart. My spirit and my soul are bigger than this five-feet-five-and-a-half-inch container I walk around in. I no longer doubt that my body is the vehicle that contains my soul.

Harvard-trained Neuroanatomist and inspirational speaker, Jill Bolte Taylor, suffered a severe haemorrhage (a stroke) in the left hemisphere of her brain in 1996 and authored her experience in *My Stroke of Insight: A Brain Scientist's Personal Journey.*

On the morning of her stroke, the thirty-seven-year-old scientist, who studied the human brain, could not walk, talk, read, write, or recall anything about her life. Over the course of hours, she became an infant trapped in a woman's body. As she tells her story and teaches from it, she clarifies that because the brain's two hemispheres are distinct, they think about different things, care about different things, and have different personalities. Our right hemisphere is all about the present moment. 'I am an energy being connected to the energy all around me through the consciousness of my right hemisphere,' says Dr Taylor.[20]

Our left hemisphere thinks in language, in a linear and methodical fashion and is all about the past and the future. This is the part that connects us and our internal world to our external world. It is that organising intelligence that reminds us to stop to pick up milk on the way home from work and lets us keep track of when we need to pay our bills. It is the voice that says, 'I am so-and-so.' As soon as we hear that, we become a separate solid individual disconnected from the energy flow around us and distinct from others. This is the portion of her brain that Dr Jill Bolte Taylor lost on the morning of her stroke. She couldn't define where she began and where she ended because the atoms and molecules in her hand blended with the atoms and molecules of her surroundings. In that moment, her left hemisphere's brain chatter went totally silent. 'Like someone took the remote control and pushed the mute button,' she explains. Alone inside her silent mind, she was captivated by the magnificence of the energy around her. With her bodily boundaries gone, she felt enormous and expansive. Gone was thirty-seven years' worth of emotional baggage, job, and relationship stresses. It was an experience of sheer euphoria.

This is the space babies live in, the space where they know no separation, labelling, or categorisation. We know this to be true when we watch a kid experience an aquarium. 'Fish!' they scream in utter delight, captivated by the colours and graceful movements inside the fish tank. An adult, on the other hand, is sorting the goldfish from the tetras from the koi, wondering about filters and plants and how to get rid of algae growth inside the tank.

But of course, physical labels have their use. There is no way I am going to arrive at a cocktail party and introduce myself as, 'Hi! I am the Universe' and risk people questioning my sanity. The bare essentials of a name, an address, and occupation provide people a framework around their experience of a person who calls herself Uma. The profound truth I know to be true for me is that I am the life-force power of the Universe experiencing and expressing itself as Uma. This truth humbles me. It confirms that the life I am living isn't just about me; it is about everyone whose lives I touch.

Cocktail parties aside, I have tried to stay connected to the truth of my Big Self, as I like to think of it, as opposed to the little egoic me. I go through life playing the roles I play—wife, mother, friend, sister, teacher, and writer. But as I perform these roles, I remind myself to stay connected to the truth of who I really am. And when Grace didn't have words, she responded to my Big Self, the energy I brought into her space. It was the purest, sweetest form of connection we could ever have shared because none of my labels mattered to her.

Theologian Søren Kierkegaard says it well: 'Once you label me you negate me.' We put people in boxes all the time. A name, a job title, an ethnic origin, a nationality. A rose doesn't have an ego, so there is no identity to pander to. As human beings, we have egos. In our limited understanding, an individual is reduced to an identity/ label. It becomes the sum total of that person who, in truth, is a magnificent spirit. Like everything else, label sizes vary; some have fancier labels and perceive that they are in bigger boxes—the seven-figure-businessman box, the Ferrari-owner box, the director-of-marketing box. Yet, how humbling it is when we realise that all those boxes come to naught when the spirit exits the body. The Ferrari box and the homeless-man box are finally equal as their cold, lifeless bodies lie six feet under.

It is useful to have a context, a framework, around people that our brains can work with, so we can slot them into our cerebral filing cabinet—Christian, dog lover, movie buff, vegetarian, etc. Labels have their place, but they are not everything. When we judge people by their labels alone, we diminish them.

Labelling and categorising can also be about mastery. Those who can label, define, and classify better are considered experts. We aspire to be like them, the walking-talking factoids. 'If I know more than you, I am better than you. And it helps me feel good,' we think to ourselves.

Living in a world that is becoming more and more competitive, I love the idea of the Zen beginner's mind—the empty mind that is simply open, curious, and engaged. This is, perhaps, best illustrated through the story of the scholar and the Zen master. A scholar approached the Zen master with a request to teach him Zen, but he rambled on and on about his extensive knowledge. The Zen master said nothing. He simply brought a teapot and started to pour tea into a cup. Except, he didn't stop pouring even when the cup was full. The tea poured into the saucer, overflowed, and ran all over the floor. The agitated scholar asked, 'What are you doing? Can't you see the cup is full?' The Zen master calmly replied, 'You are like this cup. Full and overflowing. I can't teach you. Not until you become an empty cup and ready to receive.'

Grace came into the world with an empty cup, a Zen mind. It is the great irony of life that she will lose the power of her all-knowing mind as she begins to learn the ways of the world. Instead of simply being present to a flower, she will know it as a *rose* or a *tulip*. Whereas she simply watched a fly land on the windowsill with wholesome engagement, she will learn to call it a *fly* and know that it is different from a *bumblebee*. Everything in her space was pure energy. She related and responded to everything in her world as one spirit to another, the infinite connectedness of all.

I am trying to get back to that way of living in the world, of walking in a garden and trying not to indulge in mental commentary. *Does that plant only bloom in the spring? Wonder what that flower is called?* I am simply trying to be present to life. It is a challenge trying to stay as the witnessing presence when mind chatter is almost reflexive.

From single syllable words to multisyllable words to sentences, Grace's world of knowledge continues to expand. Yet, the mystery of the unknown, the space of the divine sacred that she brought to my knowledge will always remain a precious gift.

Connect to the Essence

1. Try this experiment when you take a walk in nature.
2. Look around and really witness what you see. This means responding to everything without mental commentary.
3. Look at a butterfly, a leaf, or a bug as its pure essence. Try not to view it through the label you know it to be.
4. Reflect on the experience. Was it difficult? Easy? Did the connection feel different? Explore your reflections through art or poetry.

Chapter 23
I CELEBRATE

Grace celebrates life every single day in every possible way.

The moment her eyes open in the morning, her entire being is an embodiment of: 'Hello world! Here I am, ready to celebrate this moment, this day, this life.' She may not have the words to express this truth, but she lives it. Just being awake is a reason to rejoice in Grace's world. She dives into her day with unfettered enthusiasm.

I have known my fair share of colicky babies who cry a lot, but joy is a baby's natural state of being. They have the unique ability to flow in and out of half a dozen emotions—joy, enthusiasm, excitement, happiness, contentment, and thrill—in about three seconds!

A day is made up of a zillion moments. Often, we forget to focus on the loveliness of individual moments that make up our day. Green shoots poking out of the cracks in the sidewalk; the beautiful cherry-red feathers of a bird hunting for worms; the lazy melt of icicles from the roof of a house. They are here, but we are not. Fixated as we are on the must-get-done and should-do lists, we forget to honour the many gifts we have been given.

Celebration is not an elaborate eleven-letter euphoria for Grace. She makes each moment extraordinary by simply celebrating the ordinary. A bowl of strawberries is celebration. The warmth of sunshine on skin is celebration. Spinning until dizzy and falling in a heap on the floor is celebration. Lying on the couch and blabbing is celebration.

She is the celebration. It is her experience of life that creates the constant party.

How do we lose that when we grow out of childhood? As adults, we need a reason to revel in. New Year's Eve is cause for celebration. Getting a promotion or raise at work means celebration. Turning fifty. Winning a contract. The Fourth of July.

Celebrations have become external to us. We look to life to reward us, and when it does, we celebrate. But life disappoints, frustrates, teases, and, sometimes, passes us by. So, we wait and wait for the permission slip to have fun—a milestone, success, or special accomplishment. We have become a culture that celebrates wins. But the next day, we have to wake up and take out the trash.

Grace's celebrations spring from the essence of who she is. It is her *joie de vivre* that makes every day celebratory. A rainy day and a sunny day are all the same; one means puddles to jump in, and the other means hours of backyard fun.

When the CD player comes to life, she starts to sway and swing instinctively. Adults need a dance party. When she is out in the backyard, she can watch a bug for a full minute. We go to the Museum of Natural Science and History. She looks at the living room couch and sees a roller coaster. We go to an adventure park. In adult life, celebration has, somehow, come to be structured. It needs fine wine, company, and success.

Can we enjoy a good conversation? Can we applaud

the intention to forgive someone who has injured us? Can we celebrate waking up with breath in our bodies? Is it so hard to celebrate the feel of fresh, clean laundry as you fold towels and pillow cases? It is the celebration of ordinary moments that disappear when a loved one is terminally ill, can no longer remember who we are, or dies. Those are the moments we will miss the most and yearn for. That is the stuff memories are made of. As a hospice volunteer, I have heard family members recall the most ordinary moments they miss when a loved one dies. The smell of chili cooking as they walked in the door. The special way in which a mom arranged flowers at the dinner table. The slam of doors when a rambunctious teenager announced their arrival. Savouring a simple meal on the patio. Reading snippets from the news stories to each other on a Sunday morning.

Every life is a celebration. Just being here, living this life is a celebration. Sadness and lack and difficulty are woven into every human story, but always, always there are moments that sparkle in the darkness. Like the fresh pot of coffee a friend brings over when you are on hospital vigil. The card that arrives in the mailbox, the concern of someone who cares. Or the voice of a loved one on the phone reminding you that you are not alone.

I recall two experiences that helped me train the lens on how we ought to view success, and why we need to celebrate what is here right now.

I was working towards my Cambridge University Diploma in Teaching and Training. It was a Saturday morning class. The instructor, a lady with kind eyes and a pleasant smile, stepped in, cast a glance at us, and issued an invitation: 'Tell me about a success you have achieved in your life.'

The responses came thick and fast. Someone mentioned a novel she had just finished writing. Another talked about her doctorate degree. I spoke about writing awards I had won. Someone else mentioned excellence on the sports field. A job promotion. Getting a child enrolled in a reputed educational institution.

And, then, a voice piped up. It was that of an elderly gentleman, the oldest student in our class. He spoke about all the inconveniences he had endured that morning. Then he said, 'I celebrate being here. I made it to class today.'

The silence in the room was palpable. Everyone recognised a profound moment. We all knew a significant truth had just been spoken.

Our instructor sanctified the moment. 'All of you reached into your past and pulled out the shiniest moments. In our external pursuits and definitions of success and celebration, we have forgotten to honour the ordinary,' she said.

I have never forgotten that lesson. A few years after the classroom moment, came another. For almost a decade, I have been facilitating a weekly group called 'My Life Story' at a retirement community. One of the seniors in my group shared a lesson that had come to her through a life experience. Jean and her husband had been saving every dime they got for their fiftieth wedding anniversary festivities; they had planned to invite friends and family for a grand party. Unfortunately, Jean's husband was diagnosed with a sudden and serious illness and passed away a few months before the milestone celebration. 'Don't put all your dreams in the distant future. Do it now. Pack your bags today. Go where you can. Celebrate,' was her advice to me.

Grace reminds me of this truth every single day. She doesn't wait to get somewhere special so that she can celebrate. She doesn't think about 'When I'm old enough to ride a bike . . .' or 'When I'm big enough to swim . . .'

Her celebrations are in the moment with what she has and knows. I celebrate the wisdom this little child brings to me.

Celebrate This Moment

1. Look around you, right where you are. Let your eyes move over the objects, pets and/or people in your surroundings.
2. Think about how each of these serves you.
3. Now, close your eyes and imagine how empty your life would be if each of these objects, animals, and people were taken away from you.
4. Focus on how their presence in your life enriches you and celebrate how rich you are.
5. Think about how you can tune into gratitude for the simple things that you possibly take for granted each day.

Chapter 24

I Love to Play

Grace's vast assortment of soft toys includes a big brown teddy bear, much larger than her. A favourite in the menagerie, the teddy bear gets to ride in Grace's car seat (when the seat is propped up in a corner of the living room). She sits him down in the seat, straps him in, and, together, we take him for a pretend ride.

Another game she loves to play is swaddling her favourite doll in a pink *blanky* rocking her to sleep and laying her down for a nap. With her index finger on her lips, Grace looks at me and whispers a loud *sshhh*. We are to remain quiet as 'baby' sleeps.

Children love pretend play. Anything is possible in the realm of their fertile and vivid imagination. Not yet conditioned by limiting words such as 'can't' and 'shouldn't', they believe that anything is possible. Grace doesn't have to be sleeping for fantastical things to happen; they happen when she is wide awake.

Many afternoons, Grace is stretched out on the living room floor, legs cycling in the air, prattling away, and just having a great time. Most children don't have to work hard at play; they learn and construct their world through play.

As we grow into rules, roles, and responsibilities, we forget the art of play. Having stepped out of the sandbox of our lives and into the hard work of being adults, we abandon play. Parents believe that silliness must be squashed out of you if you want to be taken seriously. Such children grow up to be serious adults; they tend to be somewhat wary of those who are in touch with their goofy side.

Play is about belly laughs.

Play is about joy and fun.

Play is about being and daydreaming.

Play is permission for the mind to roam outside the confines of the daily agenda.

The two qualities that characterise how a child plays are 'curiosity' and 'exploration'. As Grace stacks blocks and builds a tower, she is not only having fun but also mastering hand-eye co-ordination. Apart from learning concepts like balance, size, proportion, gravity, and alignment, she is also learning how to problem-solve. She has no vocabulary for any of this, but soon, she learns that the smaller blocks go on top of the bigger ones; they have to be aligned just right so that they don't topple, and the task needs a gentle hand. The fun part is building as tall a tower as she can, then watch it teeter, totter, and, eventually, topple, blocks scattering in all directions for her to chase after, gather, and start over.

When she swings from her daddy's shoulder or hangs upside down or simply horses around, the rough-and-tumble experience is also strengthening her cognitive, emotional, and physical development.

Play signals also help develop the skill of body language. When kids get to pre-school, social skills are honed through social play—sharing, taking turns, and waiting for one's turn.

Nothing lights up the brain like play, yet many adults view play with a healthy dose of judgment. More and more, our lives have become about 'doing it right' or 'getting it done' or 'fixing it'. We meet life with a solemn countenance. As adults, we also forget that we can start over if something doesn't work right the first time. Failure does not have to be fatal.

I have heard that the opposite of play is not work, it is depression. When we don't make time for play, we disengage. Our body language becomes stiff, rigid, and conforms to the seriousness of our role in the real world. It is not uncommon for us to encounter people who return a smile with a tightening of lip and jaw muscles. Perhaps, it is an unwillingness to drop their guard. Or, maybe, they are just off somewhere else mentally.

Play is about freedom and liberation; there are no prescribed rules. And the reason we don't play enough is because we are attached to doing things by the book. Fear causes us to be reserved. *What if I fail?* We are scared of being judged, ridiculed, or laughed at. For instance, if we are in a seminar or workshop where the facilitator requests everyone to stand up and shake our bodies, tap our feet, and swing our arms to reenergise after lunch hour, it is a moment of real discomfort for many of us.

In a child's world, play is all about process. There are rules to be followed and a sense of achievement, but nothing is imposed. All outcomes are valid. What starts out as a tea party could end up with everyone flying around the room wearing pretend Superman capes. Sheets of paper and crayons, the safe beginning of an art project, could easily morph into a parade of paper hats.

If you invited a group of adults to play a game, handed one of them a teddy bear and offered a single instruction—pass the teddy bear around—there would be people in the group who wanted to know whether they should pass to their left or right; those who start to pass very quickly in the belief that speed is going to be a variable on how they perform; and yet others who wonder what happens if someone drops Teddy. In other words, adult play has an element of competition in it. It becomes more about getting to a 'destination' rather than enjoying the 'journey.' End-result, not the process.

Our inner child was well and happy when we were little, but was, soon, squashed by serious adults, and the losses and unhappiness of childhood. A good old-fashioned belly laugh is now a hazy memory.

Adults who keep their inner child alive and awake do much better in other areas of their lives, too. If you have neglected your inner child for too long, it may need some tender urging to come out and play. Explore what makes your inner child laugh and play. Don't be afraid to be silly, to laugh out loud, or clown around. Most adults reconnect with this self when they become parents. If you are not a parent, play with a child and watch what happens.

I must admit that Grace has got me back in touch with my inner child. When I am with her, I give myself permission to be silly, laugh, and pretend play. I make funny faces, hide under her blanky and play peekaboo. It is fun and feels so good to my spirit, one of the reasons why I love encouraging her parents to plan date nights so that Grace and my inner child can play.

What is fun for you? A good place to start is your childhood. When I think back to my childhood, I recall how books were my great escape. Reading was my joy. My pretend play revolved around grabbing a long cotton towel from my mother's closet, wrapping it around my waist like a sari, picking up a ruler, and teaching a classroom of invisible children. I loved to dance, too, and remember one night when my siblings and I were home with Grandma and our nanny. We ran out into the courtyard, which was bathed in moonlight, held hands, formed a circle, and danced to our heart's content. It was a precious play experience, one that shines bright in my memory.

Even in my twenties, I recall running out to the courtyard when the season's first monsoon showers drenched the parched earth. Splashing in muddy puddles made me laugh and feel a burst of joy in the centre of my heart. I remember the thrill of doing the Mexican wave when watching a cricket match between arch-rivals India and Pakistan at the cricket stadium. It was wonderful; the sense of oneness I experienced as hundreds of spectators joined in, all of us in that jam-packed stadium sweltering in the heat and having the time of our lives.

It is a good idea to loosen up, limber, and invite some playtime into our busy lives. As Judith Orloff says in her book, *Positive Energy*, 'Children have PhDs in play.' Let us relearn the art of giggling and squealing from Grace and her ilk.

Invite Your Inner Child to Play

1. Think back to when you were four or five years old. What did you love to do?
2. Reconnect with that inner child by imagining a scene from your early childhood.
3. Try to recapture your inner child's spirit which still lives within you.
4. Go out and do what that child loved to do. Was it building blocks? Dancing? Splashing in puddles? Finger-painting?
5. Do it for the sheer joy of the experience. There is no agenda.

Chapter 25

I Feel Joy Fully

Grace loves being tickled. She loves being chased around the house, running in and out of rooms until I catch her. She loves clowning around. She squeals with delight and moves her body with total abandon.

She chuckles with spontaneity when I do anything that makes her laugh. It is as if joy bubbles up from the very depths of her being and flows right out. When she sways and dips and claps and smiles her million-megawatt smile, her energy of joy rushes into my blood, my bones, and my very being. When a child is happy, there is no holding back. There is only the fullest and freest expression of pure, unadulterated joy.

When I am playing with Grace, she helps me connect with the part of me that knows and experiences joy for joy's sake. Joy that does not depend on a person, event, or outcome. It is the joy of being alive, to know and feel the wellspring of well-being.

We all have it inside us. We have just lost the map to its location. Or the switch that turns it on.

Why is it so hard to touch joy as we grow older? Where does our goofy self disappear? How did we get to a place where we have become hesitant about feeling and expressing joy?

Some of us were ordered to shut down our joy transmitters, and some of us received put-downs. Adults stared us down when we laughed out loud or rolled on the floor clutching our sides when a friend or a cousin was being silly or frivolous.

Thinking back to the days when I was a child and a teenager laughing without restraint, makes me nostalgic. Although, I do find myself in situations with friends when I am laughing so hard I can barely see through the tears, these occasions are few and far between.

Dr Brené Brown says that joy is probably the most difficult emotion to really feel. When we lose the ability or willingness to be vulnerable, joy becomes something we approach with deep foreboding. This shift happens slowly and outside of our awareness.[21]

For a good majority of us, life's labour weighs us down. The furrows between our brows become etched, the corners of our mouths turn down, and the twinkle in our eye clouded by a haze of doubt or uncertainty. Struggle, survival, and scarcity have become the heavy baggage we drag around every single day. Weighted down, we have little time or space to connect with people and situations that are our joy triggers.

We have become so focused on what is missing from our lives that joy has become the casualty. We don't feel safe enough, sure enough, or comfortable enough. We have become addicted to the myth of certainty and are terrified to live in the space of mystery. When our attention is constantly consumed with self-protection, there is little energy left for joy.

If things are going too well in our lives, we are waiting for the other shoe to drop. If my spouse is doing well at his job, the kids are healthy, and I am feeling contented with life, something terrible must definitely be around the corner. Alternately, if we have been through a traumatic event that opens us up to feeling completely, nakedly unsafe, we live in a state of perpetual fear.

Author Stephen Levine writes about a woman named Gracie in his book, 'Gracie was isolated in an obsessive vigilance. She was unable to sit still when her child was home a bit late from school, and was always "waiting for the phone to ring with bad news." She said, "Both my parents died in the last three years and, while I feel like now I'm sort of out of the deep fog of that, what I'm left with is a lot of anxiety that some other horrible thing will happen. . . . Some days I worry about what horrible thing will befall him or somebody else I love.'[22]

We feast on a neurotic diet of media-fed images of violence which fuels paranoia. We wake up each morning wondering what new calamity rocked the world while we slept. Anticipating the worst has become a way of life for so many of us. Paranoia and joy cannot live next to each other. When we feel deeply unsafe, our nervous system is agitated. Joy is experienced when we are feeling relaxed.

We have become so conditioned to negative thinking that it is not uncommon for us to fixate on airplane delays even as we are driving to the airport to fly out on vacation. We imagine the worst if our teenager promises to be home by ten and it is fifteen after. A simple sore throat has our thoughts leaping forward to chemotherapy, convinced we have throat cancer. When we are having a particularly good day with a loved one, we swallow hard and can't shake off the thought that lurks at the edge: 'Life is so good right now; it can't last.'

We have become experts at programming ourselves to expect worst-case scenarios, and when it does happen, we know that we have been prepared in some strange twisted way.

Joy leaves most of us feeling extremely vulnerable.

My husband lives by the personal mantra: don't count your chickens before they are hatched. For the longest time, I did, too, until I realised what a limiting way it is to respond to life. That is when I decided to let go and embrace joy fully in the moment. It wasn't an easy shift. It took a lot of conscious choose-again moments before I learned to lean into experiencing joy in the moment without clouding it with what-if scenarios.

When my daughter was a senior in college, she called one evening to share that she might be going on an all-expenses-paid trip to France for six weeks. I jumped and danced around the living room. I whooped for joy. France had been her dream destination ever since she had discovered the joy of baking. She had always fantasised about strolling down the sidewalks and savouring life from the vantage point of street cafes. 'Mum, we still have to wait for the college to confirm it,' I heard her shouting over my whooping. I didn't care, and that is what I told her. She was going *in the moment* and that is all that mattered.

Wisdom teacher and bestselling author, Dr Wayne W. Dyer, has taught me well. His book, *You'll See It When You Believe It*, focuses on this core principle of manifestation: what you focus on has the power to grow. When you focus on the thought that you *will* see it and, then, surrender, chances are greater that it will appear in your life experience.

The reason we hesitate to open the door and let joy

in is because we fear disappointment. Joy is neighbours with risk, uncertainty, and emotional nakedness. To soften into joy requires allowing oneself to be vulnerable. If we don't let ourselves feel joy, we believe we can stall disappointment. What we are doing is projecting our fears into an unknown future, thereby, squandering the joy in the moment.

I am sure we all know folks who, on a perfectly balmy sixty-degree day, proclaim, 'Oh, did you hear? They are talking about three inches of snow on Friday.'

Brené Brown calls this 'dress-rehearsing tragedy'. It is like being warned not to splash in a rainwater puddle for fear that the sun will shine brightly the following day and the puddle will be gone. When we worry about the fleeting nature of joy, we are already in scarcity mode. 'Once we make the connection between vulnerability and joy, the answer is pretty straightforward: We're trying to beat vulnerability to the punch. We don't want to be blindsided by hurt. We don't want to be caught off-guard, so we literally practice being devastated or never move from self-elected disappointment,'[23] writes Dr Brown.

All we have is this moment. Not the next. Nor the one after that. Joy is a string of moments meant to be fully experienced in the now. Spiritual teacher Eckhart Tolle reminds us that the ego's sole obsessions are the past and the future. It does everything it can to exit the 'now' because it believes that fulfilment or success or completion always live in the next moment.

If I had squandered the joy of the news that my daughter was going to France just to protect myself from the possible disappointment that it might not happen, it would definitely have been my fearful ego-self smothering the song of my spirit.

I find it hard to live on the fence. For one thing, I love how joy feels in my body and soul. For another, the practice of gratitude is a big part of my life. I am truly grateful for every parking spot, every meal my husband cooks for me, every breath, and every sky I wake up to, no matter its colour. A teacher of mine sent me a card I treasure. It sits on my desk and is a daily reminder: 'Gratitude expands the soul, softens the heart, and brings joy to life.' I have learned to stop and say 'thank you' in the moment. When we say thank you with a brimming heart, we are inhabiting the space of 'enough'. I must admit that I am still working on being grateful for every person who crosses my path. That is a real toughie.

I have a joy barometer in Grace. She is not afraid to giggle and shriek and dance with all of her being. When she does, her soul shines brighter. The only difference between us and a child is fear. Let us leap over that barrier and break out in soul song.

A Perfectly Joyful Day

1. Close your eyes and envision what constitutes a perfectly joyful day for you.
2. Make a list of everything you desire to create that day.
3. From exactly where you are in this moment, how can you begin to take action on each of them?
4. What inspired you today? What touched your heart? What made you grateful?

Chapter 26

I Love a Good Story

One of Grace's favourite stories involved a young boy who sets off on his boat to catch fish. All of a sudden, a furious storm tips the boat over and the basket is tossed into the waters. When he manages to swim ashore, he wanders into a forest and meets a beast who befriends him.

Grace loved all the drama and excitement we created together as we experienced the story. She loved to make the *urr* sound of the growling beast and chuckled in delight, sitting in my lap, as I rocked from side to side threatening to spill her out, mimicking the predicament the boy in the boat experienced.

We all love a good story. Storytelling has been part of the human journey from the days of sitting around a campfire and entertaining others in the circle. Then it evolved to the kitchen table format. The modern version of storytelling happens on social media as Facebook friends share the bits and pieces that make up the mosaic of their lives; bite-sized tales shared on the run.

Stories help us connect. They form the threads that weave the tapestry called the collective human experience. Stories let us know that we are all more alike than different. They help us comfort, console, celebrate, and care for one another through the ebb and flow of life.

Our homes and lives are reflections of the stories we tell and deeply care about. The objects and pictures on our mantel give people a framework for our story, a window into our lives—what we value, what beauty means to us, and what brings us joy.

Storytelling is mostly a good thing. But when we start telling stories through negative filters, our world view and experiences become distorted. For instance, if we end up being rejected at the job we interviewed for, disappointment is very real. But if we chose to turn that event into a story that goes *I'm always a failure, I don't deserve to get anything I really want*, we start to look at this life experience through a negative filter.

No matter what we are going through, the story we choose to tell determines how we experience the event. If the story we tell is rich in meaning, it gives us a sense of control over our life and inspires others. The content becomes the compass that will guide us to our next moments. Instead of blaming someone, something, or God for what happened, we extract the kernels from the story that led to our growth.

It is important to remember that our cells are listening to the stories we tell. Indigenous medicine women remind us that every part of our body has its own consciousness. Communication between the conscious mind and the physical body is real and has been used to heal self-sabotaging thoughts and beliefs. We are always telling our cells how we want to feel. Depending on the story we tell, we feel safe, happy, and in the flow of life; or victimised, miserable, and frustrated. A story can enrich or ruin our day. And when it does, there goes the rest of the hour, the rest of the day, the rest of the week, and, sometimes, the rest of our life.

It all begins with a story. You call a friend and get her voicemail, so you leave a message. The tech gremlins go to work and kill the message, so she doesn't know you called.

Hours and days go by, and you don't hear from your friend. You steam and stew that she didn't return your call. Your mind is off and running, spinning the most creative stories about a call not returned:

She hates me.

She always does this.

But she always returns Carla's calls.

I'm not going to call her. Ever.

She thinks she's the only one who's busy?

And soon, a voice message your friend didn't even receive has become a blown-up betrayal, a serious crime of misplaced loyalties.

Most of us are guilty of this. We have all fabricated fables from a place of fear. We make the other the villain because we feel victimised. Our insecurities make us feel unsafe, but instead of going within and reflecting, we blame the other for not calling us or inviting us to lunch or confiding in us. The tape that's playing in our head all the while is *Don't I matter to her anymore?* Such stories keep us wallowing in a tiny, cramped rut of self-pity.

I worked with a woman in her seventies whose entire life had become about one seminal moment in her thirties when her husband returned home from work one evening and told her that he wanted out of the marriage. For the next forty years, she continued to carry the hatred, anger, and bitterness of that announcement and all the ways in which she was cheated out of a life he had promised her when they exchanged vows. She clung to her story tenaciously and refused the feeblest attempt anyone made to help her rewrite the script of her life. She traced every health challenge, financial storm, and unsatisfying career choice back to the moment when this man had successfully ruined her life. Abandonment became her theme song.

Contrast that with another senior, Ruth, in her eighties, who lost her twenty-year-old son decades ago in a horrific crash caused by a drunk driver. Years later, dealing with her husband's worsening dementia, Ruth was still full of smiles and sunshine. She always spoke about how young Rick had chosen her to be his mother (that was her belief) and the gift of twenty glorious years with him. She had worked hard on forgiving the driver and was at peace as a result of the choices she had made after her son's death.

Both tragic storylines, but uniquely scripted takeaways by the main players.

Children don't ruminate. It is a lesson they teach us over and over again. One evening, I watched Grace as she eagerly crawled on all fours to get to the basement, but her mama had other plans. When her mama scooped her up off the stairs, Grace set up a loud wail. And when she was set down and the child gate firmly shut, she stomped and stormed off to her nursery as her mama and I called out to her from the living room. Less than twenty seconds later, Grace emerged from her nursery cradling Boo, her favourite furry toy, grinning from ear to ear. The only evidence of her displeasure moments ago were the tears that still clung to her pretty lashes. Gone was the fury, the rebellious outburst at a thwarted wish.

She was telling no stories about it. It was already consigned to her past. Here was a fresh moment—Boo cradled to her chest, pure pleasure back in her life.

In that split second, Grace brought home a very powerful lesson for me. Storytelling is the mind's way of holding on, of making the other wrong (not once, but a thousand times), of wanting to exact revenge, of living in the past.

What happened, happened. We can't 'unhappen' it. All we have are two choices—we can either stay stuck or we can move forward. The reason so many of us prefer the former option is because we mistakenly believe that our anger is our way of holding on to the injustice of what happened. We are convinced that is where our power lies.

If we stay angry or think that we have power over our offender (never mind that our offender is probably on a sunny beach somewhere in Florida), we only end up hurting ourselves.

The reason we become attached to retelling our story is because it helps us enlist others' sympathy and gain votes that we are right, and this awful thing was done to us. If we stay stuck in victim mode, aka the comfort zone, we have to take no responsibility for our part in what happened; so, there is no need to change, no discomfort of growth to be endured.

We can choose to stay trapped in victim land or we can put our stories to good use. Bishop T.D. Jakes of The Potter's House says it best: 'When you hold on to your history, you do it at the expense of your destiny.' The only stories we can create begin here and now. The stories that shaped our lives have already been enacted; they can't be changed (except in our interpretation of them). Therefore, if we invest all our energies in what happened yesterday, we are not available for today.

I can't say that I have enjoyed every lousy thing that happened in my life, but I certainly try to stay connected to the wisdom that things happen not *to* me but *for* me. I do make an honest effort to find the lesson in my disempowering stories to empower myself and others, to find a better way to be, to love, and to live.

Too many of us use our stories of *I had a terrible childhood* or *He betrayed me* or *She abused me* or *They turned their backs on me* to define who we become in the world.

Every wound contains a wealth of wisdom. The question is: am I using my stories to build a safety net for my failures? Do I blame my inability to hold down a job on my father who was a wanderer and never stayed at a single job for any length of time? Or am I going to bless the very things I hated as they happened to me because they grew and expanded my soul? Can I commit to recognising and intentionally changing patterns so that I stop repeating what I didn't like about my life?

Stories can be as narrow and limiting as a rut or vast and expansive as the sky. We get to choose the stories we tell. You and I are as big as our stories. The basic plotline is given to us, but we get to flesh it out and adorn it. Do I want to weave an inspiring thread into the fabric of my story? How can I tease out the tangled stitches and make a new pattern? Is my attitude the trimming that will enrich the ending? Can I embroider my story with the spirit of a blessing? These are decisions we get to make. The meaning and purpose of our stories determine whether they will fly or die.

When it rains on your parade, you can whine about it or give thanks that the drought ended.

Grace shows me how she lets go of stories all the time. In the blink of an eye, she is onto the next story, one that makes her smile and brings her joy.

The gift of Grace is a powerful thread in the tapestry of my life.

The Power of Story

1. Bring to mind a story you are telling about a life event that presents a challenge. You see yourself as a victim in this story.
2. Now imagine that you are an author. Write the story as if it were happening to a character in your story. Watch how the dynamics shift.
3. Play with possible choices and endings. It opens your mind to explore the different possibilities for all the characters engaging in this drama.
4. Experiment with motivations, personalities, opinions, and beliefs. You just might feel a sense of compassion and understanding for the choices the characters in your real life made.

Chapter 27

I Am Free

As I watched Grace tumbling on the grass, I began to ponder the meaning of freedom. Grace surrenders to the impulse to just *be* and *do* whatever her instinct calls her to. She chases Em, the family dog, and tries to grab her tail. If she is in the mood for stories, she rushes to her bookshelf and grabs a book that we can read together. If the sun and wind invite her outdoors, she runs to the closet for her shoes. If she is bursting to release the energy coiled up inside her, she uses the living room furniture like a jungle gym. In short, she simply responds to life's invitations from one moment to the next, fully relishing what brings her joy.

The older we grow, the further this kind of freedom recedes from our lives. We build schedules and structures and begin to function within self- or society-imposed boundaries. The problem begins when those schedules and structures morph into a cage called life where we start to pace, unfulfilled and restless. Over time, seeing no way out, we make the cage our comfort zone.

We wake up, shower, dress, and drive to work. We check emails, dial into conference calls, and duck in and out of meetings. There is the punctuation mark called lunch, in the middle of the day, where we are constantly answering emails. Digital devices keep us company at lunch. We finish work, drive home, sink into the couch, check more email, tune into a Netflix show or adrenaline-arousing news. This becomes life as we know it.

Thankfully, freedom is creeping back into our vocabulary. People are waking up to how terrible bondage feels, whether they are experiencing it in economic, corporate, marital, or mortgage terms. Our spirit just wants to be free. But, somehow, we have bought into the notion that more equals happiness, and we can't seem to get off the treadmill that promises the lifestyle which will bring us more.

Is it really possible to be free and have a good life? We mistakenly believe that a good life is tied to struggle and sacrifice and money.

Doesn't it follow that you have to trade your soul if you want the big house, best private schools for your children, and the cosy retirement fund? You begin to believe that you have to be a part of the corporate rat race if you want the materialistic luxuries when your heart truly yearns to work with differently abled kids or start a non-profit for cancer survivors.

People are straining at life's leash. We feel the choking pressure of being strangled by life as it *should* be done versus life as we *wish* to experience. All too soon we are sinking, gasping for air. Access to more resources also means access to more temptations. It is the gateway to a life of excess.

Everyone hungers for meaning and purpose. We find ourselves wondering: *why am I in this rat race? There must be more to life than bills and mortgages!* A lot of the time we have chained ourselves in ways that keep us stuck. When our belief that we have to work hard and struggle to make a living drives our actions, we suffocate. The very act of internalising that belief takes away freedom.

What are some ways in which we squander freedom? How do we stay locked up in our little self?

By believing that we have to do it alone. By saying yes when we really want to say no. By looking far ahead and living in a fear-ridden imaginary future instead of attending to what is right in front of us. By supersizing our doubts and thumbnailing our dreams. By marrying our jobs and divorcing our families. By focusing on our body at the expense of our soul.

'Freedom is a state of mind that you have to develop. Or more accurately, and paradoxically, Freedom is a way of being that you have to surrender to with great discipline,' says Danielle LaPorte, bestselling author of *The Desire Map: A Guide to Creating Goals with Soul*, international speaker, and entrepreneur. Conformity and achievement are early lessons we imbibe and find really hard to shake off. Turning it on its head could be as dramatic as working on a Sunday or following your natural impulses to sleep in, bike, hike, and stay in your fuzzy slippers and a comfy bathrobe on a Wednesday. But the experience of freedom is intimately interwoven with self-love. As long as we are tied to the apron strings of another's approval, we will never gift ourselves the freedom to follow our heart.

Grace is comfortable in her own sense of self. She is intensely and fully engaged in *this* moment. She walks the journey of life at her own pace, trusting in the rightness of her rhythm. She gives all of who she is— love, laughter, and light—and is open to the experience of what shows up in return.

Lately, I have become more mindful of the word 'freedom' and what it means to me. There was a time when I believed that my happiness was closely tied to my dream of becoming a New York Times bestselling author. If a big publishing house offered me a solid contract with plenty of money, and my book sold a million copies, I would have made it. The world would be so proud of me, and so would I.

Now, I choose to be happy with or without the dream the world says I should have as a writer. When I align with the spaciousness of freedom, I take on marketing activities that are fun for me—as much fun as the writing. Chasing after the dream that the world dreams for me is a mistake. Would I like being a NYT bestselling author? Sure. Am I going to sweat and stress over it? No way. I am having such a good time speaking about my book, sharing it with diverse audiences, and signing reader copies without stressing about my Twitter feed and my platform.

I know in my heart that I live in a Universe that conspires on my behalf. Does that mean I get everything I want? No. I usually get what I need. And, sometimes, not getting what I think I need is a reminder not to stick my fingers in the Universe's business.

It is a freedom born of faith, of surrendering to an infinite Universe that handles billions of stars and galaxies. How hard is handling my life, in comparison? I work on relinquishing the need to control the outcome and, then, am able to savour the sweet taste of freedom.

I am warming to the idea that freedom is a state of mind. That is how Nelson Mandela survived three decades of imprisonment. Mandela's mind was free to roam beyond the prison bars and taste the possibility of a free South Africa. 'As I walked out the door toward the gate that would lead to my freedom, I knew if I didn't leave my bitterness and hatred behind, I'd still be in prison,' he said.

Fortunately, more and more adults are beginning to redefine freedom. A new possibility is worming its way into contemporary consciousness—less is more. At least, it is in the lives of those who have been burned by the reality of a life of more or nagged by the hollow feeling in their soul that there is more to life.

What does freedom mean to me?

Freedom is knowing I don't have to do life alone; I am always supported by the force that makes the Universe pulse.

Freedom is feeling connected to the part of me that knows my journey.

Freedom is letting go; it is surrendering my small-self's agenda to the grand vision of my Soul.

Freedom is faith over fear.

Freedom is doing less and being more.

Freedom is the feeling I experience when I see the sunbeams, dew on grass, and raindrops cradled in a leaf.

When we begin to view freedom through this lens, it becomes expansive and readily available to us. And it doesn't always have to involve the exchange of dollars.

Grace is a free spirit; we can be, too. All we need to do is reconnect to the child within who knows what it means to be truly free.

The Freedom Wheel

1. Get a sheet of paper and draw a circle in the middle.
2. Write the word FREEDOM in the middle of the circle.
3. Draw lines radiating from the outer periphery of the circle, like sunrays.
4. On each ray write what freedom means to you. For instance, to wear clothes I really like irrespective of my body size and shape, to speak my mind in a crowd, to have a few baby-free hours every Sunday, or to spend three hours doing nothing.
5. Make a commitment to bring at least one experience of freedom into your life every week.

Chapter 28

I Believe Everything Can Be Fixed

Grace and I were spending time together one evening while her parents were out on a date. We started off by playing with paints, colouring clouds, flowers, and birds. All of a sudden, the blue crayon snapped in two. Without a moment's hesitation, Grace held it out to me, and said, 'Fix it.'

In her innocent world, I could just take the two broken pieces, put them together, and make it a whole crayon, good as new. I had to gently explain to her that the two broken pieces could not be fixed.

Another day, she and I were playing in the backyard when she decided to pluck a flower off a plant. When she was done gazing at the flower from all angles, she handed it back to me, and said, 'Fix it.'

This time she wanted me to stick the flower back into the plant. In her innocent mind, the flower would fuse right back into the broken stem.

'Everything that is broken can be fixed' seemed to be Grace's simple mantra in life.

It led me to a moment of reflection, to wonder about all the things that are broken in an adult life, and how easy life would be if we could simply fuse them back together, to have them go back to how they used to be.

Broken relationships. Broken promises. Broken dreams. Broken commitments. And broken hearts.

Things break. People break. It is a fact of life.

I reflected on Grace's response to the blue crayon. She didn't want me to get her a new crayon; her instinctive response was to look for a way to fix it so it could be made whole. Do we come into this world with an intuitive sense that things and people can be fixed, mended, and healed? It is something to think about.

Sometimes, life needs breakage. If relationships didn't break, we may settle for much less. What if a spouse stayed in a marriage that was broken beyond repair, entertaining the delusion that it can be fixed? It happens more often than not. Breakage forces us to let go and turn our attention inwards. It lets us ask the questions that lead to something new, some new way of being or seeing.

Like Grace, we come into this world whole. And, then, we are broken. We are like fine china in the rough hands of people who don't know how to treat us with the tenderness and delicacy we deserve. So, we chip and crack, dent and damage. We walk through this world, our fabulous self turned into taped-up glass held together on a wing and a prayer. As we journey through life, people bump into us and further crack what is already brittle. Every slur, every comparison, and every awful, mean thing people say to us renders us more and more fragile.

That is why some marriages and relationships must, eventually, crumble. When the brokenness of two people is shattered beyond repair, all they can do is gather the shards, toss them in the trash, and make a brand-new beginning.

We do everything we can to not break. This is probably why we hanker after perfectionism. But perfectionism is boring. Our flaws and foibles, those individual fault lines we inherit as legacy from our parents, make us unique. How we pick up the broken bits of our lives— the death of someone we love, the letting go of a toxic friendship, the dissolution of an unfaithful marriage, the harsh reality of infertility—and piece together a new mosaic of meaning is what determines how we show up in the world.

I love the lines in Leonard Cohen's song, *Anthem:*

> *Ring the bells that still can ring*
> *Forget your perfect offering*
> *There is a crack in everything*
> *That's how the light gets in.*

Why must we deal with broken promises, dreams, and hearts? My heart shattered into a million pieces when my beloved sixty-eight-year-old mother died in January 2009. It took everything I had to put myself back together. The shattered me is gone forever. Who I am today is the pieced-back version whose motivation and meaning stem from my reconfigured self. I can never go back to being who I used to be. Equally, that girl could never be who I am today. I had to be broken.

Every breakthrough is preceded by a breakdown. Even the situations that can be fixed are irrevocably changed. People can fix themselves, too, but it depends on how we find meaning in the broken fragments of their lives. Even more important is how willing we are to let our brokenness show through so that others can see those scars and connect to the truth of their own brokenness.

For example, when a friend shares her guilt about not looking forward to having her mother at Thanksgiving dinner because of their difficult relationship, I have a choice. I can either take on a holier-than-thou attitude and preach to her about forgiveness, or I can be real and let her know that I have harboured similar feelings in other situations, too. When, in that moment, I allow her to see my humanness, it is a moment of true connection. This truth is best reflected in the Ethiopian proverb which translates to: 'What you conceal cannot be healed.'

Take a divorce, for instance. Messy and ugly as it can be, it can also mean a whole new beginning for the two people involved. If they took what broke in the relationship and examined those psychological shards, it could be the starting point to a new journey in awareness. The magic begins to happen when they ask powerful questions: *what was I unwilling to give in this relationship? What do I need to heal in order to be whole? What lessons have come to me through this experience?* But it is entirely possible that one or both of them may stay at *why me? Life is so unfair! He is so selfish!* and nothing would change. They would simply carry the same unexamined baggage into their next relationship.

Having gone through breakage and pain of some kind—death, divorce, child sex abuse, or domestic violence—we extract the wisdom from those terrible experiences best when we are willing to share our story. In so doing, we open our heart (and our arms) to someone in similar shoes who is desperately seeking a thread of connection. In my opinion, that really is how we turn pain into purpose in a way that is meaningful because we can use our pain to serve another.

Any relationship that breaks is changed forever. Spiritual teachers tell us that, sometimes, a couple comes together to learn from each other through a karmic contract. When the contract comes to a natural conclusion, there is a break-up which signifies the end of the spiritual arrangement they made for growth and learning. If the couple stays connected and is able to maintain a friendship, the relationship takes new form. If not, they part ways and begin new journeys. How they choose to view what happened and how it changes the choices they make determine the lessons learned or not.

When we paper over our brokenness and pretend we are whole, we start to wear masks. We haven't dealt with the wounds, so we experience the psychical equivalent of walking through the woods with lacerations on our arms. Every twig, leaf, or tree branch that touches the exposed area triggers the discomfort. It is a constant reminder that the wounds need attention. When we accept our brokenness and mend our wounds, we have an opportunity to become whole. Not perfect, but whole. And that is our true reason for being here; for me, to connect with you through the common bridge of brokenness. So, we walk towards each other and 'walk each other home' as spiritual teacher Ram Dass says.

In losing my mother, I had to learn the language of grief. To learn it, I first had to feel deeply into my sadness and heal it. I had to walk in the shoes of a bereaved daughter before I could serve others who are floundering in the confusion of grief.

Grace will be broken in ways through which she is meant to serve the world. My hope and prayer are that she doesn't hide from her brokenness or become defined by it. I hope she will find the courage to hold it up to the light and reflect on how best to heal it and, thus, heal her world through it.

The Puzzle

1. Toss all the pieces of a puzzle and let them scatter.
2. Look at the puzzle pieces as they have fallen to the ground.
3. Move and shift them around to make new patterns. Watch how they always don't fit together but create a symmetry all their own.
4. Reflect on a situation in your own life where the pieces have scattered in a way that is causing you discomfort.
5. Write in your journal about the new patterns you see emerging from this situation: new insights, lessons, and ways of being and seeing.

Chapter 29

I Own Up

Once upon a time, a beautiful blown-glass dog lived in one of our cabinets. The day Grace spied it, she wanted it. Two-year-olds don't know their own strength, so the fragile canine didn't last long in Grace's hands. The dog still lives in our cabinet, its head placed alongside its body.

Grace still loves the dog and points to it. Each time she sees it, she remembers, 'Dog boke.' When I ask her, 'Who broke the dog?' she responds with complete honesty, 'Gracie boke dog.'

No shame. No blame. No judgment. Just a simple statement of fact.

I am no idealist and know this phase isn't forever. It won't be too long before her mommy walks in to referee a squabble, and Grace will point to the other kid in the room as the originator of the conflict, innocence pooling in her big hazel eyes.

But she is not there yet. She knows how to own up.

She is still on the cusp of learning that there is a right way and a wrong way. That some choices will get her into trouble, and other choices a pat on the back. She has no need to defend her actions because she isn't threatened by anything. She is still not aware of cause and effect, choice and consequence.

The moment we learn that bad actions have bad consequences, we also learn to defend and protect ourselves. It starts innocently enough.

He broke it.

She hit me first.

She is telling a lie.

Owning up isn't cool. Owning up doesn't feel good. Owning up doesn't feel safe.

How many of us grew up with parents who promised us that we wouldn't be punished if we simply told the truth? My guess is, not many.

Children jump right into experiencing life without thinking about consequences. They love to colour outside the lines. Adults feel the need to corral them in, for fear that they will grow to be wild and unmanageable without regularly administered doses of discipline. Parents hate tantrums because they believe it is a poor reflection of their parenting skills. A tantrum is simply a child's way of releasing negative energy. They know how to do this instinctively, and don't stuff emotions that don't feel good, as adults do. They need to get it out of their system to feel good again.

However, punishment for a tantrum sends a loud message to the child: 'If you behave in ways that we deem inappropriate, you will suffer the consequences.' But a child, being a child, has an instinct to break free, break rules, try new things, and test boundaries. When punishment follows, the child gets the message that she/he must self-protect. The easiest way to self-defence is to blame the other.

With people and situations pushing our buttons, whether intentionally or not, we have ample opportunities to practice the blame-and-shame game.

Blame becomes part of our arsenal, deeply etched into our mental groove as a response when things don't go our way.

Belligerent bosses, insensitive strangers, friends with their own wounds, and the rights and wrongs of relationship dramas hone our blaming skills.

Blame is one of the biggest adult games we all engage in. We get so good at playing this game that we begin to see ourselves in an I-can-do-no-wrong light, no matter the situation. J.K. Rowling says, 'There is an expiry date on blaming your parents for steering you in the wrong direction; the moment you are old enough to take the wheel, responsibility lies with you.'

For most of us, victim land is a good place to inhabit. We enter that space as a way to protect ourselves: 'No, Mommy, he hit me first.' As we grow older and life presents people and circumstances that challenge us, we grow a little more comfortable in victim land. We drag in a comfy couch there, set up a bookcase, and settle down. Then, we bring in a favourite drink and a friend who receives our constant whining with patience and begin to live there. Over the years, it becomes home: safe, familiar, unthreatening. We sit on that couch, rehashing the same stories, seeing ourselves at the mercy of a brutal, unjust world. In time, our vocabulary revolves around: 'If he would just . . .' or 'If she would only . . .' or 'If only they wouldn't . . .'

I used to visit with a senior who had become a permanent resident of victim land. She had had a rough childhood. Her marriage had ended abruptly in an acrimonious fashion. She and her daughter were on cordial terms, but she rarely showed up to visit with her mother, restricting contact to what was absolutely necessary.

I was empathetic to her situation, but even I couldn't stretch my boundaries beyond a point. Over the eighteen months that I visited with her, I tried a variety of strategies to gently nudge her out of victim land. But she loved it there. It was always summer in her corner, but when her relatives, ex-husband, or friends visited, they dragged in mud and slush from their relentless winters and she hated how they spoiled her summer. Life was very cushy; she didn't have to lift a finger except to point in blame.

As long as we make someone else responsible for our pain and misery, we don't have to take responsibility. Owning up is hard. It is hard to turn that finger towards ourselves and ask the tough questions: 'What am I not owning up to in this situation? Why am I being triggered by this?' It is what therapists call an 'internal locus of control' as opposed to an 'external locus of control'. The locus of control is the extent to which people believe they have control over the events in their lives. Developed by J.B. Rotter, it is a set of thirteen questions used to figure out whether your locus of control is internal or external. A person with an internal locus of control believes that they can influence events and their outcomes, while someone with an external locus of control blames outside forces for everything. The former correlates with happiness, success, and initiative; the latter correlates with control issues, anxiety, and depression.

Owning up is not easy. It means accepting that you messed up and need to clean up. It means allowing yourself to be vulnerable and inadequate and declaring that to a spouse, friend, co-worker, or sibling. It means accepting that your triggers are your own and that only you can work on them.

Our greatest transformation is only possible when we are willing to venture into our dark spaces and slay our dragons. When we stop running, turn around, and look the dragon in the eye, we begin our hero's journey.

Like everything in life, it takes constant practice. We need to work the 'owning up' muscles. Alvaro Pascual-Leone, professor of Neurology at Harvard Medical School and one of the world's foremost neuroscientists says: 'From a brain perspective, every time we do something we are more likely to do it again and every time we stop ourselves from doing something we are less likely to do it again.'[24]

We need to create families and communities where it is safe to make mistakes and redo life. Because as long as we fear the consequences, we will take the easy way out and peg the blame on another.

We can all own up to being on this imperfect human journey—isn't that the truth!

Grace will grow into a responsible adult who knows how to take responsibility for her acts of omission and commission as long as she has the emotional wiggle room. As long as she hears the consistent message that mistakes are milestones down life's long road. And as long as she knows that failure is simply feedback.

Cleaning up Your Day

1. As you go to bed at night, allow your mind to reflect on the choices you made through the

day. The intention here is a gentle review, not self-flagellation.

2. Use these two questions to review your choices: a) What could I have done better? b) How could I have been kinder?

3. If you feel some resistance come up, get curious about the fears that stop you from wanting to do and be better.

Chapter 30

I Need to Throw a Tantrum

When Grace wants something *now* but doesn't get it (because a caring adult who knows better says a firm no), she throws a good old-fashioned tantrum. In that one instant of thwarted gratification, her tender little body morphs into an erupting volcano. She cries, stomps her feet, and expresses her extreme displeasure loud and clear.

Most toddlers I have known engage in this behaviour, some more often than others. When I was a young mother, my instinctive response to a temper tantrum was to walk away. I would say to my toddler sprawled on the floor, 'I'll be in the bedroom. Come find me when you're done.' I have no idea how I knew to do this or where the wisdom came from because I know today that it is the only sane thing a parent can do in that situation. If we are unable to disengage from the teary toddler, it's so easy to get triggered. But I digress.

I have always pondered the question: How does a two-year-old know to indulge in an impressive attention-getting performance? All the parenting books tell you how a child's behaviour is modelled on what she observes in the adults in her environment. Children don't listen to what you say; they do what you do. They are perfect mimics. But I am yet to see a full-grown adult sprawled and screaming in a grocery store aisle because their favourite cereal was temporarily out of stock.

Toddlers experience complex feelings and express emotions by ripping paper, stomping their feet, and yelling when they are mad. With a bundle of synapses firing crazily, new neural pathways in construction create chaos in their emotional highways.

Somehow, none of these answers satisfied me. Something was missing until I asked a spiritual teacher and found an answer that resonated with me.

'How does a toddler know the choreography of a tantrum?' I asked her.

'Kids are in touch with their bodies,' she responded. 'Unlike adults,' she added.

That got my attention. This was delicious, rich.

She went on to explain that when a toddler's want is denied, they feel severe emotions: frustration, anger, and sadness. The flood of negative feelings rushing into the body does not feel good to them. Their innate wisdom lets them know they need to 'shake it off'. That is exactly what a toddler does: the foot-stomping, hand-flailing, screaming-at-the-top-of-their-lungs routine, aka the emotional meltdown.

When I watch Grace five minutes later, I see the picture of perfect serenity and joy. Having expelled those icky feelings from her body, she dives into the next thing that brings her joy—cuddling with a soft toy, climbing the couch, or tapping a foot to whatever is flowing out of the stereo system.

The storm has passed. The sun is out again. All is well in her world.

When I heard the spiritual teacher explain a tantrum this way, it made perfect sense. I also recognised there are great lessons here for adults who deal with a child's tantrums.

When we see a tantrum coming, we need to prepare—just as we do when a hurricane threatens to blow through town. We need to pay attention to the alerts coming our way. Even as we prepare to face a hurricane knowing that it won't last forever, we know that a toddler's temper tantrum, too, shall pass. Even as we see the rage building—the tightening jaw, widening eyes, and look of fury—we take evasive action and remove breakables from the vicinity, or they may become convenient objects to hurl. We refrain from judgment. Just as we would never label a natural disaster an 'inconsiderate' hurricane, we choose not to call the child a 'bad' girl or boy. We don't need to rush headlong to fight it by restraining the toddler's arms and legs in a bid to stop the drama just as we don't yell at the hurricane, 'Stop it or you will be in trouble.'

We wait, knowing that a hurricane isn't forever. It will eventually blow through, and, soon, calm will prevail; so will a temper tantrum. It is, however, necessary to help toddlers develop words to express what they are feeling so that they have a way to channel their feelings instead of engaging in damaging behaviour.

Unfortunately, most tantrums are subject to judgment, ridicule, or threatening measures. When that happens, the child internalises the message: *I am bad* or *I am not lovable*. Sometimes, instead of reassuring the child that it is safe to express, letting them know that they can sit down with their favourite soft toy and calm down, vent, and let those emotions out, we teach them to hold it in. Enter the beginning of neuroses. That child grows into an adult—you, me, and everyone we know— who doesn't know what to do with the emotional ferment within or how to contain it.

These are some of the beliefs we live by:

> *Emotions are bad.*
> *I am not supposed to feel.*
> *People who show emotions are weak.*
> *If I express how I feel, I will be seen as an out-of-control freak.*
> *The better I am able to hold it all in, the stronger and more in control I am.*
> *It is okay to be angry, but it is not okay to be sad.*

We try to remain in the middle space where we are not too sad or too joyful. We believe that we are in control when we keep our sadness contained. We are also in control when we are not being too happy because, God forbid, if you are too happy, something terrible is bound to come along and shatter it.

Grace, on the other hand, experiences pure, unadulterated joy when she is splashing around in the bathtub, making a mess of a bowl of ice cream, climbing the kitchen counter to grab a cookie from the jar, grabbing the dog's tail, or assembling a puzzle. She also experiences complete sorrow when told that she can't watch another episode of her favourite show, *Bubble Guppies.* Unbridled anger when she is denied a cookie right before dinner. Tenderness when she applies lotion gently on my cheeks, one of her favourite things to do. She feels it all because that is the only way she knows how to be.

Emotions are inner messengers. Every emotion comes bearing an important alert. They draw our attention to the things we need to respond to. Anger lets us know that a boundary has been violated. If we didn't feel anger, we would let people walk all over us. Sadness tells us that it is time to let go. Grief lets us know that we lost something, and we could do nothing about it. Fear urges us to take action.

As adults, we are expected to show restraint. We can't punch our boss in the face because our request for a raise was turned down or stomp our feet in the library because the movie we wanted to watch this Sunday is checked out.

You can, however, deal with your feelings in healthy, acceptable ways. No one is going to stop you from yelling and cussing in a parking lot. Or from crying your eyes out because your teenager is being an insensitive jerk. Or from giving yourself a timeout from everyone and everything wrecking your sanity. To calm down, take a bubble bath, go for a walk in the woods, hit the gym, or curl up with a delicious murder mystery and a margarita. Writing a letter and giving your rage a safe space to exit is also a healthy way to defuse anger. Or learning how to engage in hard conversations with an open heart. All of these help release the energy you are carrying. Unfortunately, most of us have never been taught how to do this. We have had no healthy role models for emotional expression.

I am personally delighted that emotional intelligence is now being recognised as a vital tool in the human's survival and success kit. According to the 2009 Dictionary of Psychology, Emotional Intelligence (EI) or Emotional Quotient (EQ) can be defined as 'the ability to monitor one's own and other people's emotions, to discriminate between different emotions and label them appropriately and to use emotional information to guide thinking and behaviour.' George Bernard Shaw once advised, 'Better keep yourself clean and bright; you are the window through which you must see the world.'

As I watch Grace, I realise this truth all over again. It is all good. It is all okay. Foot stomping makes foot tapping possible. If you don't scream your frustrations and let the wind carry it away, you will forget how to squeal in delight.

Grace is my guide. She constantly reminds me of what it truly means to be human.

Play Emotional Detective

1. The next time you are angry, notice the sensations in your body.
2. Begin to understand what you are experiencing. Is it mild irritation? Full-blown rage? Annoyance? Reflect on the boundary that is being violated.
3. What is the story you are making up about the event? It could be: 'She doesn't care about me' or 'I never do anything right' or 'Everyone thinks I am stupid.'
4. How does rewriting the story make you feel?
5. Do the same with envy, sadness, fear, and grief.

Chapter 31

I Am Safe

Grace went to her first musical when she was twenty-six months old. Not surprising, given her parents' love of theatre and active involvement in everything from page to stage. Her dad is an actor who also writes screenplays; her mom designs costumes.

They invited me to go with them to see the musical, *Oliver Twist*.

When the lights went down, and the stage lit up, Grace was entranced—for all of ten seconds. Then, she wanted to run off and explore, unmindful of the fact that she was in a large auditorium full of strangers.

To honour her need for freedom, her dad and I took turns at making regular excursions outside. It felt like we were creating our own version of entertainment for Grace. As I held her in my arms and stood on the sidewalk, she happily watched cars zip down the street. Then we spent some time gazing at the flowers and stopped to look at the poster of the musical. She was chatty, happy, and, clearly, relieved not to be shushed every three seconds just because she wanted to climb on a chair and shout out a loud 'Hi!' to the kids on stage.

The first time she and I went outside and the doors closed behind us, I realised that I couldn't open them from the outside. For a few seconds, I felt panic streak through my veins. We were locked out and my cell phone was in my bag sitting inside the theatre.

As I circled the building and walked around to the other side hoping to find a way in, Grace continued to hum and repeat words to herself, perfectly content with life.

She felt safe. She knew that she was safe. She was with an adult she trusted. She never doubted that I would find my way back inside, back to her mom and dad.

Soon, we got to the other side of the building and, sure enough, the entrance doors to the building were wide open, and we walked back inside.

This little incident made me ponder the concept of safety, what it means to us, and how it impacts us. Sure, Grace felt safe because she was with an adult she trusted and felt safe with. If I had left her on the sidewalk and walked away, there would have been no more safety for her. As adults, what do we attach to that we believe will keep us safe?

We have been raised to internalise the belief that safety is external to us. We place our faith in people and places.

If I have a stable career—law, medicine, engineering— I'll be safe.

If I make enough money and have a well-padded nest egg, I'll be safe.

If I live a good life and contribute and tithe and serve, I'll be safe.

If I drink red wine, eat broccoli, and run three miles every day, I'll be safe.

If I play small, never speak up, and make my partner feel good, I'll be safe.

Think about people you know. Chances are, you know someone who lives life by one of those mantras. Someone who played by the rules and *still* lost the game.

There is no insurance for life. Life is about adventure, uncertainty, mystery, failure, falling down, getting it wrong, getting back up, and getting it right.

My own life experiences and nights of soul-searching have brought me to the truth that safety is internal. The longer we pretend—and, sometimes, believe— that we can find safety in the perfect insurance policy, educational degree, income, or life partner, the more vulnerable we become. The illusion must crumble, and we will all come to the truth in our own way. Highly regarded in India, my Cambridge University Diploma in Teaching and Training counted for nothing when I started a job search in America. All the money in her bank and the best treatments didn't keep my mother from dying of cancer in a short span of eight months. Becoming an entrepreneur and following my passion is all about sticking my neck out and risking myself every single day. But I am so invested in my soul-calling that I am also invested in the faith that will accompany me on this journey.

It is funny how we let this idea of safety play out in our lives.

We are ready to move in with a partner but vacillate when it comes to commitment, aka marriage. It is almost as if a live-in arrangement has an unspoken exit clause—it helps us feel safe. Exiting a marriage is messy financially and emotionally, and it involves more than just the two main players.

From seat belts to lawsuits, we live in a culture that breeds dread. All the fine print on every document is driven by the fear of litigation. It seems acceptable to advertise the most potent medication for everything from an ordinary headache to erectile dysfunction, but the disastrous side effects are deeply rooted in fear. It is like: 'We told you so! Don't blame it on us if you drop dead.' To me, it seems like an organised safety net approach that smacks of terror.

'The discomfort associated with groundlessness, with the fundamental ambiguity of being human, comes from our attachment to wanting things to be a certain way,'[25] writes Pema Chödrön, an American Buddhist nun, in her book.

I work with people who are grieving a loss. There is no insurance against loss. Attempting to be safe is like cupping your hands to scoop up water and believing you can hold it there. Those I work with believed that they had password-protected safety and yet couldn't control a thing in their lives.

Some couldn't keep their children safe.

Some couldn't keep entire families safe.

Some didn't know how to protect a job, a home, a spouse, and a business into which they had invested their heart and soul.

My friend Therese Tappouni, counsellor, author, teacher, and a mom, who lost her eleven-year-old son expresses this idea of helplessness eloquently in her book:

'Perhaps the deepest wounding in grief is our realization that we are not in control and we are not safe. We've spent a lifetime preparing for every possibility, protecting ourselves and our loved ones by buying safe cars, making sure we wear seat belts, stopping smoking, getting regular medical check-ups, submitting to vaccinations, living in secure neighborhoods, taking herbs and vitamins, and doing crossword puzzles to avoid Alzheimer's. The list is exhausting. Lately, even grocery stores provide hand sanitizer to kill germs on our shopping carts. Despite all of our precautions, warning systems, and protections put in place, this *thing* still got through.'[26]

We have embraced the idea that if we just follow all the rules, we will be safe. But that is denying our very humanness. We are meant to grow and there is no growth in safety. Growth always happens outside our comfort zones. Our ego will do everything in its power to protect us, but our soul is all about expansion. So many people suppress their passion to paint or sculpt or design for fear that their talents won't put food on the table. Entrepreneurship is not for the faint-hearted. Every single day requires you to find the courage that your work matters, that there are people in the world who need your services/products, and you can find a way to make it work.

How do we navigate this journey that seems fraught with danger? How do we feel safe and keep our loved ones safe?

Not by taking seasonal flu shots.

Not by avoiding difficult conversations.

Not by pretending we won't ever die.

There is no universal answer to this life question. I have not conquered fear, nor do I harbour the illusion that I have to conquer it. Fear is a powerful and terrorising beast, but also an ally. Life brings me situations that present fear, and I do feel the fear. But, then, I go to my faith to anchor myself in the waters of serenity. I can only share with you how I deal with it. When I feel the fear, I sit with it, question it, and try to discover what it is really about. I till the garden and shake up the soil of old issues that still drive me, trigger me, and frighten me. Sometimes, I catch it right away, and other times, I have to wait because my ego is stubborn and unrelenting. But if I am patient, I eventually get to it. Once I do, I can anchor in what always serves me: my lifeline to the Divine. I know that I am held, I will be held, especially, during difficult times. It is about coming back to my centre where I am always safe no matter what is going on in my physical world. For instance, when clients dry up as they sometimes do, and my mind begins to spin the old tales about how risky entrepreneurship is and what was I thinking, I connect to the thoughts that remind me of the truth: all the clients who have been served, all the money I have made through those sessions, and the joy my work brings me every single day.

Fear, doubt, and danger exist in the future. When I travel there and get caught in their frightening grip, I consciously remind myself to embrace the not-knowingness of life. When I take off and leap weeks and months into the future, I need to have the presence to parachute back to the present. If I hit the pause button, I know I have everything I need in this moment.

'If you can remember the present moment, you can be less subject to anxiety,' write Susan L. Smalley, PhD, writer, and activist, and Diana Winston, a mindfulness teacher and writer, in their book. 'Anxiety needs a future (and is often fueled by the past),' they add.[27]

The other favourite tool I use several times a day is gratitude. I expand my attention towards what is right and give thanks for it. Gratitude is a high-vibration energy. By focusing on abundance and being thankful for that abundance, we create more abundance. Research lets us know that feeling grateful boosts the immune system, floods the body with feel-good neurotransmitters, and increases happiness levels.

We live constricted by fear because we deposit our safety in people even though we know that no one is perfect. When we place our faith in what is perfect and what can and will support us no matter what, we feel grounded in safety.

Through her unquestioning trust in the adults she loves, Grace feels safe. She knows nothing about human brokenness. And when she does, I wish for her an enduring love affair with the Divine. It is where she came from. It is who she is. It is where her safety lies.

Your Safe Space

1. In this exercise, I invite you to create your own safe space. Close your eyes and take yourself to a space where you felt very safe as a young person—it could be your grandma's kitchen, your mother's lap, a chapel or temple, or the arms of a loved one. If none of these spaces denote safety any more, create your own.
2. Visualise a space. It could be the ocean, the mountains, a cave, or a beautiful garden. See the details, smell the fragrances, and hear the sounds in this space. Surround yourself

with things that are cosy, comfortable, and safe. A teddy bear from your childhood, a favourite shawl, essential oils, prayer beads, a journal and pen . . . anything that supports relaxation.

3. Feel the muscles in your body breathe in relaxation and complete peace as you take yourself to this space. This is your haven, your sanctuary.

4. Any time life feels overwhelming or threatening, you can travel to your safe space and feel relaxed in minutes.

Chapter 32

I Love Me

Like many children I have known, Grace went through the delightful phase of dramatising a minor scratch on her arm just so she could sport a colourful Band-Aid; she also made a production of picking the perfect one. Sorting through an assortment of favourite cartoon characters, she, then, proudly brandished the injured body part. But every time she got a boo-boo, real or not, she also loved having an adult kiss it and make it go away. As a natural extension of this, she started to kiss her own boo-boos with such affection. It is endearing to watch a two-year-old's uninhibited expression of self-love. Spontaneous, unembarrassed, unprompted.

It reminds me of all the boo-boos I have carried over the years, all the times I held out my figurative arm for others to kiss it and make it better. And when people ignored my boo-boos or refused to do what I believed they ought to do to heal me, I stayed there, arm outstretched, stubbornly needy.

The best example of this is Sister Valeria, the nun who taught me Psychology in college. After years of being broken on the inside and smiling on the outside, I suffered a moment of utter weakness, burst into tears, and confided in her. I described the messiness of my home life with an alcoholic father who wrecked my sanity. Sister Valeria opened her heart to me and loved me generously. In a very short time, I grew addicted to that love, starved as I had been for a long time. Soon, she became the custodian of my confidences and the source of my love, attention, and validation. Any time I caught Sister laugh with or hug any of her other students, red-hot jealousy coursed through my veins.

She was officially appointed my boo-boo kisser.

There were other Sister Valerias in my life before I learned the hard lesson that it was *my* job to love me.

What I didn't recognise was that I was only a fraction of her large world. Sister was a busy person with classes to teach, papers to grade, and convent and community duties. But if she failed to notice me or smile at me, the sun wouldn't shine on my day. This kind of behavior has a term in Psychology: transference. I was clearly looking to receive from Sister what I didn't receive from the adults in my life. This became a pattern I repeated in other unhealthy friendships, too. It took a lot of self-reflection and hard work to break this habit so that I could learn to fill my own love tank.

Many of us do this, especially, in our romantic relationships. We bestow on our significant other the terrible burden of loving us the way we want to be loved.

He is responsible for fixing my happiness.

She needs to be available to me, no matter what.

If only she would love me more, I could feel better about life.

We go through life appointing our boo-boo kissers, and if they don't kiss where it hurts, we resort to blaming, shaming, guilting, and jilting them.

What if we started to kiss our own boo-boos and

made them better? What stops us from nurturing our own selves? Why does the very mention of the word 'self-love' cause us to break out in hives?

A big reason is that we grow up receiving conditional love from people who have been wounded themselves. That kind of love doesn't feel wholesome or genuine. How can it? The source of that love is imperfect. If we really understand that we were loved and parented imperfectly, and we will love and parent imperfectly—no matter how noble our intentions—we would lay down a great burden.

Some of us grow up receiving gallons of love; some of us, pints. Some, veritable drops, and others, an occasional trickle that soon runs dry. Love runs dry when our grades aren't up to par, we don't make the soccer trials, we can't tinkle on a piano like our cousin can, and we don't ever understand the profundity of a quadratic equation.

So, we grow up feeling judged, flawed, and stunted. How can we feel good about who we are when we are always hearing the words 'You won't ever' or 'You can't' or 'You'll never be as good as . . .' Every verbal put-down confirms and underscores our smallness. Our worthlessness takes root and begins to thrive. The critical voice that takes up residence in our head keeps us from following our dreams, from knowing we have inherent value, and feeling like we matter. This voice becomes the self-appointed boss and calls the shots as we step into our teens, twenties, and adulthood. Inspirational humourist, author, and performer of the one-woman show, *Shopping as a Spiritual Path*, Terri Tate named the voice in her head 'The Vile Bitch Upstairs'.

I'll never be good enough.

I'm not thin enough, smart enough, good looking enough, talented enough, rich enough, qualified enough . . .

And, soon, this giant shadow begins to affect everything we think, say, and do. Our lives become driven by those four awful words.

I am not enough.

And life feeds us more experiences, people, and opportunities that solidify our personal lie. With every disappointment and every blow dealt, we shrink smaller and think smaller.

That is when we begin to look to 'The Other' in our life to make us feel lovable and worthy. And for a while, The Other does—in the honeymoon phase of the relationship. We buy into the grand illusion, the universal lie that saccharine love conquers all, and we can finally feel whole because we have found The One whose sole purpose was to incarnate and give us what nobody else could.

It takes many years, some hard knocks, and rude wake-up calls for us to smell the coffee. We aren't meant to go out with the figurative begging bowl, we aren't meant to look for love outside of us, and we aren't ever going to find that bliss of love if we don't learn how to grow it in our own hearts.

Perfect love is a lie. Imperfect love is true love. That is the only flavour available, even if we learn to make it ourselves.

Do I love myself well now? Most of the time. Enough for me to look at my reflection in the mirror, gaze deeply into my eyes, and mouth the words: 'You are precious and important, and you deserve all the abundance the Universe is sending you today. I love you as you are in this moment, and I am proud of you.' But every once in a while, I forget and travel to the Land of Disappearing Love and scarcity becomes my story. It takes a while to pivot back, and when I do, I reflect on where I was feeling wounded and how I didn't hold myself.

I do like me today. I didn't for many years. It took a lot of healing, learning about my human-divine Self, and loving myself enough through my worst mistakes so that I can be my own authentic self in the world.

Do I like all of me always? No. Do I have bad days? Certainly. But do I beat myself up? No. Because I no longer buy into the belief that my personality is bigger than my essence. I know that the core of who I am is pure love and light, and I touch that space within me often enough. Especially, when I am having a not-so-good day. Enough to know that on the days that I am unable to rise up and be my better self, I can hold myself with compassion, knowing that this, too, shall pass, that tomorrow is another day, that the sun will still rise, and all will be well.

A lack of self-love is at the root of all our problems. We rush around trying to fix all that is wrong in our lives—money problems, spouse, kids, job, weight, and relatives. Little do we know that self-value and self-love are the places where most other issues are mired.

If we don't feel worthy, we make choices to garner approval and acceptance. We squander the gifts of authenticity.

If we don't believe we deserve it, we undervalue ourselves and remain underpaid even if we excel at what we do.

If we buy into the notion that we are not enough, we live by others' standards and crush our dreams into oblivion.

If we believe that we are broken and flawed in some irreparable way, that is how we engage with the world, and we attract broken, flawed people who don't feel good about themselves.

If we feel we have to keep on giving to have value, we give from a dry tank and are constantly depleted.

It bears repeating—everything goes back to self-love.

For me, the journey towards self-love began with the huge *aha!* moment that nothing is really broken inside me. My light is as bright as it was the day I arrived here. It has just been veiled over—a thousand veils wrapped over the light, dimming its brilliance. My job is to gently unpeel one veil after another to find my way back home to my true self.

It is not about addition; it is about subtraction. I can read every single self-help book there is to read. I can attend every personal development workshop I can find. I can enrol in all the self-improvement seminars I know of. But if I don't do the inner work, the work of unpeeling layer after layer, I cannot manifest the life I wish to create for me, my loved ones, and those I serve.

How do we go about this task of loving ourselves? I can only share with you what worked for me and invite you to find your own path.

I cleaned up my connection with Spirit.

I started to take stock of what I liked about me.

I began to step out of self-absorption and connect with others' lives, their worlds.

I dove into a richer understanding of what it means to be a spiritual being having a human experience.

I practiced self-compassion—the Self who held the little self when I made a mistake and turned it into a milestone.

I used joy as my inner compass to tune into people and experiences that are a good vibrational match for me.

When you really get that you are a tiny spark of the Divine, it shifts your understanding of self-love. If the Divine isn't flawed or wrong, how can you, made of the same elements as the Divine, be?

A child knows this instinctively. That is why they don't judge, compare, divide, and separate. They love with a pure wholehearted innocence. They love you and me and themselves. They love enough to know that as long as they kiss their own boo-boos, they are in good hands.

Grace opened a world of wisdom for me by that one powerful act: kissing her own boo-boo.

Ask a Wise Being

1. Think back to the worst mistake you have made and how you judge and blame yourself for that mistake.
2. Imagine a wise grandmother, a loving being, or the most caring friend you have ever had speak to you about that mistake. What would they say?

3. Take that wisdom and speak those words to yourself, holding the image in your mind of yourself as a five-year-old boy or girl. Most likely, your offensive act as an adult has its roots in a need that went unmet in childhood.

Chapter 33

I HAVE ALL THE TIME I NEED

When it is time for me to head home after spending an hour with Grace, I usually say, 'I'll see you on Saturday, okay?' Grace looks at me, her innocent hazel eyes brimful of the certainty of love. She has zero understanding of what I just said.

To Grace, it matters little when I will see her next. She has no idea of what 'next Wednesday' or 'tomorrow afternoon' or 'later in the day' mean. Time is a gloriously elastic, stretchable, and never-ending expanse. Think about it. That is how you and I used to be. There was a time when we had all the time in the world, all the time we needed, all the time to be and grow in beautiful ways.

Time is of no consequence to Grace because she hasn't learned to assign any value to it. In the magnificent state of freedom that she lives in, *now* is all there is.

What about me?

When I am preparing to take leave of her, there is already a sense of: 'Oh no! My time with her is coming to an end.' When I know that I will be watching her on the Saturday her parents are going out on a date, anticipation starts building in me from Friday as I think: 'In less than twenty-four hours, I'll get to hang out with my favourite little person.'

I am an adult for whom time is a shifting, ever-changing phenomenon. If my to-do list has more check marks on it, it is a productive day; I take a pleasant end-of-the-day feeling to bed with me. If I have wasted time in just one or two time-consuming pursuits which don't contribute to my passion or purpose, a feeling of stale regret comes over me.

There is so much judgment around time. So much criticism, scarcity, so many ways to measure what we do with it.

Time becomes something we grasp onto when there is a sense of a joyous event coming to an end. There is no such thing in Grace's world. Here and now is all there is. She is happy to throw all of herself into wherever she is right now because the past and future don't exist for her. So, when I say goodbye to her, she is not thinking: 'Oh no! Uma's leaving already.' And when I am on my way to see her the next time, she is not working herself up feverishly with: 'Only fifteen minutes till Uma gets here!'

Time is a human concept. We have seasons, clocks, calendars, planners, and all the latest e-reminders that help us track the twenty-four hours in our lives. With the aid of all these devices, we are still time-challenged.

Consider some of the phrases we randomly repeat in our daily lives.

I am running out of time.

Time waits for no one.

I am racing against time.

We are on a time crunch here.

Like most things in life, time has come to be all about lack and scarcity. It matters little that we have all been given the same twenty-four hours. As Lynne Twist says in her well-loved book, 'Before we even sit up in bed, before our feet touch the floor, we're already inadequate, already behind, already losing, already lacking something. And by the time we go to bed at night, our minds race with a litany of what we didn't get, or didn't get done, that day. . . . What begins as a simple expression of the hurried life, or even the challenged life, grows into the great justification for an unfulfilled life. . . .'[28]

Time management seminars and books like *The Four-Hour Work Week* have reached an all-time popularity because we all want to know how to milk more out of every second in our day.

Questions to ask, consider, and reflect upon:

Is there really too little time or am I cramming way too much into my day?

Do I need to get all of it done today?

What are the consequences if I don't?

Am I feeling distracted and, therefore, less focused?

Am I giving my attention to the things on my list that move me in the direction of what I truly care about?

I have found it useful to adopt the fifteen-minute rule. In the world of multitasking, my attention threatens to scatter in a zillion directions—an upcoming telephone interview, blog posts to write, emails to respond to, and courses to outline. In this crazy scenario, reading, which is my first love, sometimes gets sidelined. So, I allow myself the luxury of fifteen delicious minutes. I stop everything else. It is just the book and me. Phone calls go to voicemail, the laptop is turned off, and I get more reading done with the fifteen-minute rule.

The fifteen-minute rule works well for most things:

fifteen-minute segments to answer emails, write, engage with folks on Facebook, meditate, and walk around the block for a breath of fresh air. I have come to realise that it is not about the amount of time; it is the focused attention to the one thing I am doing. All those days I attempted to multitask, I was simply deluding myself that I was getting more done when my concentration was actually splintered amongst three tasks: talking on the phone, typing an email, and checking things off my calendar.

When I explained my fifteen-minute rule to the seniors in my weekly group, even they thought it was a great idea. 'I'm going to try this,' said one. 'I miss reading. I used to read a lot, but have gotten sidetracked by doctor's appointments, therapy, going to activities, and exercise that I just don't read anymore. But fifteen minutes? Sure, I have fifteen minutes to read.'

Time is the big, fat, modern lie. When we are wedded to the idea that all good things are soon going to end, we bring a grasping quality to the beauty that we experience in the world.

The vacation is almost over.

This delicious book I can't put down is coming to The End.

The party I planned, prepared for, and anticipated is almost to its end.

In some ways, we live in constant dread of losing the things we love the most. An undercurrent of ache travels below the most pleasurable experiences we consume. When that happens, there is a holding back. We are unable to give all of ourselves to that experience because we fear that it will soon be over, and we will be left with only the memories of what was.

If every child you know carried that feeling to the amusement park and on every ride that they went on, they could never squeal in glee, shriek in delight, and flush red-cheeked with the colour of pure pleasure.

What if we approached everything in life as if joy were forever? How might it change us? How might it reframe life experiences for us? If we bring a fullness, a ripe appreciation to bear on life's every gift, that gift becomes infused with joy. You only get out of anything what you give to it.

On the contrary, if we attempt to control or manipulate our experience with *I won't give all of myself to it* or *I'll be disappointed when it's over*, we peg our joy meters way below what is possible.

If downing a carton of Triple Chocolate Fudge Sundae is judged as addictive behaviour, why shouldn't cramming way more than is possible into the hours of a day be any different?

Subscribing to the idea that more is good is probably based on the belief that doing more equals feeling more of. We are in awe of people who are magical multitaskers. *He gets so much done. His energy is amazing. She has so much on her plate, but she has this ability to do it all without breaking a sweat.*

In the meantime, our internal candle is burning down, dripping messy wax all over our soul. What if our to-do list comprised of six items instead of sixteen? What if we could pat ourselves on the back for what we checked off that list instead of agonising over what didn't get done? What if we had a to-be list which included:

1. Be kind to three people
2. Remember to thank life for all the awesomeness of today
3. Breathe mindfully
4. Look one person in the eye and have a conversation
5. Mindfully savour every sip of a beverage.

Time is what you and I make of it, do with it, and bring to it. We could live with the constant lament of *I don't have enough time to do what I like*. Or we could consciously choose to create the life we desire with the same twenty-four hours you and I have been given. And that could be as simple as bringing mindfulness and intentionality to what needs to get done.

Grace's timeline is really simple. Here and now is all there is. She dives into it with all she has and creates a past and a future that are filled with fun and life.

It is high time we did the same.

Check Your Calendar

1. Open your diary or the calendar app on your phone.
2. Go over the last thirty days and review where you spent your time.
3. Make a list of all your activities and the amount of time you spent on them. You could make categories like Job, Health, Relationships, Self-Care, and Creativity.
4. Review if you have been investing time in what truly matters to you.

5. Make a conscious decision to reorient your priorities so that you begin to live a life aligned with your values.

Chapter 34

I Colour outside the Lines

When Grace assembles a snowman from a card template, she sticks his carrot nose facing the opposite way from how it is usually done. When we play the Memory Game with a deck of cards, she matches her own unique pairs. A dog could be paired with a parakeet, a hat with a school bus, and a bell with a hippo. When she is colouring, her sky is canary yellow, her grass crimson, and trees are a bright shade of purple. When we set up to play Toss the Rings, she finds a variety of uses for the sticks, none of which involves planting them firmly in the ground so we can toss the rings around them.

In Grace's world, there is only one rule: have fun and do it my way. No matter what she is doing, she gets to make up the rules, and they are all good as long as they contribute to the grand purpose—fun. Any rule that obstructs fun is tossed out.

As we grow older, fun is sucked right out of our lives. I once heard a mother complain that her ten-year-old daughter laughed too much and too loud. When she was encouraged to dig deeper to figure out the source of her discomfort around her daughter's behaviour, she tapped into her belief, 'If you are seen as flippant, the world doesn't take you seriously.' This belief was the beginning of a story that was playing in the auditorium of her mind—her daughter missing out on lead roles in school plays, being passed over for the best jobs, and being dismissed as childish and immature. Tangled in that terrifying prospect, the mother was trying to turn a naturally bubbly, effervescent, and fun-spirited kid into a sobered-up, socially acceptable version.

Rules. Rules. Rules. There are too many of them for our own good. So well-trained have we become that we learn to dwell comfortably inside man-made fences, rarely venturing out for fear that we will make mistakes, face disapproval, and be alone. If we happen to stray outside the lines, we don't really know what to do or how to be because we are well-conditioned by a family/cultural formula.

My maternal grandmother's home was a place where orderliness and sobriety of behaviour were prized attributes. It was no place for kids because spontaneous shrieks of delight were met with stern glares. We mostly had to keep it down. Do kids even know how to do that? The grandkids who were seen and not heard received favours, suitable rewards for toeing the line. Others like me, who could rarely resist the thrill of a dare, were understandably unpopular. When Grandpa was in his home office entertaining someone important, the house felt like a tomb—clean, quiet, and almost sinister with silence. There was no room for fun.

But kids just want to have fun. When they engage in any kind of activity, pleasure is the only agenda. Watch an adult engage in an activity and you will notice that 'doing it right' or 'being the best' becomes the goal; just the thing that takes the fun out of the activity.

Well, can paying the bills be considered a fun activity? It is a matter of perspective, I guess. We pay for experiences we deem as enjoyable. We have to pay a car loan but driving around and seeing new places is fun. We pay for cable but think of all the hours of pleasure we experience watching our favourite shows. Playing *Angry Birds* on a cell phone is fun, too. So, when it comes time to pay those pesky bills we can connect with gratitude for all the perks and privileges we enjoy—the car, the television, microwave, cell phone, hot water. We can choose not to whine about giving our pay cheque away.

And how about having a little fun when you are vacuuming the rugs, soaping the dishes, or even scrubbing the toilet bowl? In her book, *Be the Miracle: 50 Lessons for Making the Impossible Possible,* author Regina Brett introduces the reader to Valerie in the essay titled 'We all do the same things. It's how we do them that makes the difference.'

Valerie cleaned restrooms for a living at the Charlotte airport in North Carolina. Anytime a customer walked in, she called out cheerily, 'Welcome to Valerie's Restroom.' Valerie's motto was: 'Don't worry, Pee happy.' Always smiling and singing, Valerie entertained every woman who passed through her restroom with these words: 'You are my sunshine, you are my sunshine'; 'There are plenty of seats for you'; 'No line, no waiting, no waiting, no line'; 'It's very important that you get a seat in Valerie's Happy Restroom. This is where you go to pee happy.'

A woman who cleaned public restrooms for a living all day long found a way to inject fun and spirit into a job most of us would call thankless and mind-numbing. I love how the author describes Valerie's attitude. She

writes, 'You've got to admire her joy for life in what—
pun intended—could be a pretty crappy job.'

It is a perfect example of colouring outside the lines.

In her spiritual memoir, author Anne D. LeClaire
writes:

> One day I was invited to speak to a second-grade
> class about writing. I began talking about the
> importance for writers of not being afraid to speak
> up. It is the first prerequisite, I told the class. And
> then, as a warm-up exercise, I asked them to make
> the sound of their favorite animal. Within seconds,
> the room erupted. Hoots, howls, barks, meows,
> baas. And within minutes, they were at their desks
> writing a story about their animal, beginning with
> the premise, 'What if . . .'
>
> One child wrote, 'What if a tiger kept a human
> for a pet?'
>
> I was struck by one thing that morning: unlike
> many older students, not one child resisted writing a
> story. No one disclaimed that she was better at math
> or that he was better at soccer and wasn't good at
> English. Watching them, I was reminded of a study
> out of the University of Michigan that Madeleine
> L'Engle wrote of in her book Walking on Water. The
> study found that in first grade the students asked
> 80% of the questions, by fifth grade they asked 50%,
> and in high school only 20%, the rest instead coming
> from the teachers . . .
>
> Then after I spoke to the second graders, I gave
> a talk to an audience of three hundred adults. Still
> inspired by the morning's experience with the
> children, I decided on the spot to duplicate the

exercise. Again I spoke about the importance of writers not being afraid to use their voices. And then I asked everyone in the audience to make the sound of their favorite animal. I was greeted by a silence so complete it felt as if everyone had stopped breathing. I understood. It was too risky. Many of us are afraid we'll be the only one barking like a dog, screeching like an owl.[29]

Colouring *inside* the lines is not all bad. It says that you are attentive to details, you are methodical and focused, you are someone who enjoys the process and can ensure that you create something that is a wonderful end product. You have respect for quality.

It is when we start living inside that box, the confined space we allow to become our mediocre life, that rules begin to suffocate. It is necessary to occasionally tweak the rules so that our spirit's innate creative spark can thrive. If the very thought of breaking a rule brings on paralysis, at least play with a comfortable level of discomfort. If straying from a committed diet and exercise regimen scares the bejesus out of you, learn to enjoy the occasional single scoop of your favourite ice cream, or take a break from the gym. If you are looking for love and terrified to go on a blind date, begin by asking a friend to set you up with someone she knows.

What might colouring outside the lines look like?

It could be attempting something that you normally wouldn't. Like getting in the car and driving without a destination in mind. Or speaking your mind when that voice inside you is afraid to emerge. Taking an afternoon nap when everything in you is screaming to crank out a few more emails. Or turning your cell phone off for a couple of hours just to breathe and unwind.

It is basically changing the rules in how you experience life. Break a pattern, open the door to unease, and savour life in a varied texture.

For some of us, it is writing that book—a terrifying prospect because it raises the decibel level of the doubter; saying the big Yes to someone you have been dating for aeons; quitting your full-time job to paint; or visiting a friend who is in hospice.

Colouring outside the lines is scary, but also liberating. It proves to us that we can, that we are safe, that it is okay to make mistakes, and that the world won't reject us as imperfect jerks. And maybe, it is about saying 'I don't care' to what is no longer true. Like friends who love you as long as you live within the acceptability box; a spouse who approves as long as you play small; a boss who feels competent as long as you are willing to hide your light; an adult daughter who promises to love you as long as you meet her needs.

I could never have written four books (one still in my laptop's hard drive) without being willing to colour outside the lines. I didn't know the answer to any of these questions:

How do I write 75,000 words?
How do I even know when a chapter ends and another begins?
Who will publish my book?
What do I have to say that hasn't been said before?

But I had to show up and get the pages written. If I had stayed inside the lines, waiting to be ready until I had all the answers, I would never have written a single word. Writing is about exploration, creativity, and self-trust.

When I ask Grace to draw a flower, she never says she doesn't know how to. She grabs a crayon and a sheet of paper and begins. There is power in that intentional act. She and the muse dance together on that page. In doing so, she lets me find my own rhythm.

Go Where You Fear to Go

1. Identify something you would love to do but have been afraid to pursue. Painting, writing, making craft, working with teens . . .
2. Ask yourself what you can do to venture beyond your comfort zone. Maybe, a simple first step could be visiting a craft store and poking around. Or sitting down and writing your vision for how you would like to make a difference in the lives of teenagers.
3. Boldly take the first step. And then the next and the next as you watch how fear is a fog that keeps you from moving forward. As you do move onwards, the fog begins to lift, and your path becomes clearer.

Chapter 35

I Can

When Grace comes to our house for a sleepover, my husband and I usually accede to her request to go to the neighbourhood park in the evening. At the park, Grace always wants to go on the biggest slide, swing from the tallest bars, climb the scariest loopy, twirly contraptions, and attempt everything the older kids are doing. She is such a daredevil. Game to try everything that kids three times her age and size attempt, she mostly does just fine.

She barely even glances at the toddler swings and slides. They don't present any kind of challenge. Everything about her declares the 'I Can' attitude. She doesn't, for a moment, look at the older kids and think: 'Gee! They're way taller and bigger than me.' Nor does she look at the toddlers in the park and go: 'Hmm, that's where I belong. I'll just play with those kids my size and stay safe.'

She simply follows her inner compass which must be saying: 'That looks like fun! Go for it! You can do it!' And she takes off, never questioning or doubting the truth of it.

On the other hand, many of us adults live life by a series of 'I Can't'. Or we say 'I Can' to all the wrong things for all the wrong reasons—*I can work fourteen-hour days and stay healthy* or *I can make this relationship work even though he treats me with little respect* or *I can keep saying Yes to everyone in my life and stay sane.*

Some of my clients tell me that they fantasise about being an entrepreneur but work at dead-end jobs that demoralise them. My job as their coach is to awaken their long-buried dreams and passions. For some people, the very word 'dream' is dead as the Dodo. It is buried so deep that it becomes an archaeological excavation to uncover it and feel around its forgotten edges. But they eventually get there. As they connect with their heart's desire, their body language changes, a sparkle lights up their eyes, and they sit up straighter as they reach into the far recesses of imagination where possibilities beckon.

Moments later, they wilt. The sparkle dies. Shoulders slump. Long, heavy sighs emerge with the tremulous whispers of 'I can't'. Their soul's desire which lit them up a moment ago is obscured by fears, doubts, and limiting beliefs. In a single session they make the emotional transition from sparkle to slump. I have run into this more times than I can count.

As I help them dig deeper, road blocks surface.

I don't have the skill set.

I don't have the time.

I don't have my husband's support.

I don't have the necessary contacts.

And brick by brick, they demolish their fragile dream.

As adults, we slowly lose the creative power to imagine possibilities. Give a child a sheet of paper, tell them to make a hat and, in most cases, you won't hear them say 'I can't' or 'I don't know how to'. A child's world is all about out-of-the-box thinking. It is a world that hasn't been contaminated by conditioning. Anything is possible. Everything is possible.

E.E. Cummings once said, 'Once we believe in ourselves, we can risk curiosity, wonder, spontaneous delight or any experience that reveals the human spirit.'

I remember a time when my husband was cleaning out a particularly dusty shelf in our basement. Prone to congested sinuses, he had taken the precaution of wearing a nose mask. Grace was with us at the time, and I watched her observe him very carefully. Moments later, she picked up the other mask lying around, placed it over her nose, and declared, 'Nose Hat.' There was much laughter which followed that declaration. But in that moment, when Grace combined two completely unrelated concepts and forged a uniquely creative possibility, the 'Nose Hat' was born.

I am so proud of my husband for saying 'I Can' when we had the opportunity to move to the US after living in India for the first four decades of our lives. It was a tough 'I Can' to declare in one's forties. And he declared it in the face of statements from friends and family who said, 'You can't. You shouldn't. Not at this stage in your lives.' I think of all the rich cultural experiences and education we would have missed out on had he said, 'I Can't.' It was a case of imagining, then creating a whole new possibility, a new beginning for his family in a foreign country.

The 'I Can' attitude takes courage, determination, and self-belief. You have to be willing to enter the arena, unattached to the eventual outcome. If things hadn't worked out for us in America, we would have parachuted back home to the known and familiar, but, at least, we gave it our best shot. But we had to invest in our self-belief, not in others' doubts. Therein lies the satisfaction of any life experience. If our attachment is that the outcome be successful, we can't enter the arena from a place of positive intention. The key is to show up and give it all you have got. No matter what happens, every experience leaves you with gifts if you are open to the possibility.

The fear of 'I Can't' is inextricably tied to 'I Can't fail'. For so many of us, failure is about loss of control. It is why we stay close to what we know, what is easy, and what doesn't challenge our comfort zone. Because when we fail, all those slumbering demons inside us wake up and start to holler.

Did you really think you could?

Who do you think you are?

You've never been good at anything.

Told you, I saw it coming.

We are ruled by those demons. We bow to them. They keep us in line. Unfortunately, that means the death of our dreams.

'I Can' is about following the inner fire. It is about not knowing how things will pan out but simply being willing to take the next step and dealing with what is right in front of you—even if it is just saying a definitive hush to that hollering demon.

Grace meets the world from the space of pure possibility. The wholesome being that she is, she has no voices in her head . . . yet. So, she leaps and dives into every adventure that comes her way—whether it is baking blueberry muffins with Mommy, clambering onto the kitchen counter fearlessly, or assembling a gingerbread house. It is all about exploration. It is all about fun. It is living life because it brings her joy.

Let us take a leaf out of that glorious Book of Life. Let us start by saying the small 'I Can' until it becomes a habit that expands our horizons. Let us meet life with the attitude of 'What am I getting out of this?' instead of 'Will it make me look bad if I don't get it right?'

A toddler may be a jumble of confusing impulses, but there is a pint-sized world of wisdom there that we, as adults, can learn from.

What's Your 'I Can't'?

1. Identify a habit in your life which you find difficult to change. It could be not waking up early in the morning, a lack of commitment to exercise, or eating potato chips when you are sad.
2. Set a small goal you know you can achieve. Wake up ten minutes early. Park your car farther from the building where you work and force yourself to walk more.
3. Notice when you achieve the goal. Set yourself another small goal.
4. As you achieve small goals, you develop your self-confidence muscle. Every small goal achieved reinforces your 'I Can'.
5. Now, go for some bigger goals. Wake up an hour earlier. Get a gym membership. Eat a salad daily.

AFTERWORD

A newborn is placed in the arms of her/his mother, and it is the birth of a momentous occasion. A world of responsibility opens up. But it is also a sacred moment when two souls, who committed to teaching and loving one another, begin their journey.

Babies have the power to bring out the best in us. Yet to be marked by cultural and societal conditioning, they arrive in our lives as pure beings of love and light.

It is my sacred intention that reading this book will help you look at a baby with eyes of wonder and curiosity and ask the question: 'What are you going to teach me today?' For as they grow, they help us grow, too, in ways we never imagined possible. As they take baby steps and learn to walk and talk, they guide us on our path.

May every baby that blesses your life be a gift of joy.

Acknowledgments

My deepest gratitude to . . .

. . . my Divine team . . . I am grateful to be a vessel through which you channel perfect inspiration into the world.

. . . my husband, Girish . . . your unwavering support and love mean the world to me.

. . . my daughter, Ruki, whose love of literature gives us both the gift of hours of great conversations.

. . . Chris and Tiff who blessed me with the gift of Grace.

. . . the members of the Schaumburg Writers Group whose generous critiques helped me shape this book. Writing is definitely a little less lonely with a tribe that has your back.

Notes and References

1. Anne LeClaire, *Listening Below the Noise: The Transformative Power of Silence* (New York: Harper Perennial, 2009).
2. Michael Mendizza, 'Sensory Deprivation and the Developing Brain', Touch the Future, https://ttfuture. org/files/2/pdf/mm_sensory_deprivation.pdf.
3. Brené Brown, *The Gifts of Imperfection: Let Go of Who You Think You're Supposed to Be and Embrace Who You Are* (Minnesota: Hazelden Publishing, 2010).
4. John O'Donohue, interview with Krista Tippet, On Being, 17 September 2009, https://onbeing.org/ programs/john-odonohue-inner-landscape-beauty-3/.
5. Krista Tippet, 'The Inner Landscape of Beauty', *On Being*, 17 September 2009, https://onbeing.org/ programs/john-odonohue-inner-landscape-beauty-3/.
6. Thich Nhat Hanh, 'Clouds In Each Paper', *Awakin.org*, 25 March 2002, http://www.awakin.org/read/view. php?tid=222.
7. Zalman Schachter-Shalomi and Ronald S. Miller, *From Age-ing to Sage-ing: A Revolutionary Approach to Growing Older* (New York: Grand Central Publishing, 1997).
8. Debbie Hampton, 'The Multitasking Myth', *The Best Brain Possible*, 14 September 2014, https://www. thebestbrainpossible.com/the-multitasking-myth/.

9. American Psychological Association, 'Multitasking: Switching costs,' *American Psychological Association*, 20 March 2006, https://www.apa.org/research/action/multitask.aspx.

10. Christine Rosen, 'The Myth of Multitasking,' *The New Atlantis: A Journal of technology & Society 108* (2008), under 'Changing our Brains,' http://faculty.winthrop.edu/hinera/CRTW-Spring_2011/TheMythofMultitasking_Rosen.pdf.

11. John Medina, *Brain Rules: 12 Rules for Surviving and Thriving at Home, Work, and School* (Washington: Pear Press, 2008).

12. Brené Brown, *Daring Greatly: How the Courage to Be Vulnerable Transforms the Way We Live, Love, Parent, and Lead* (New York: Avery Publishing, 2012).

13. Brené Brown, *The Gifts of Imperfection: Let Go of Who You Think You're Supposed to Be and Embrace Who You Are* (Minnesota: Hazelden Publishing, 2010).

14. Emma M. Seppälä, 'The Real Secret to Intimacy (and Why It Scares Us),' *Psychology Today*, 5 September 2012, https://www.psychologytoday.com/us/blog/feeling-it/201209/the-real-secret-intimacy-and-why-it-scares-us.

15. Brené Brown, *Daring Greatly: How the Courage to Be Vulnerable Transforms the Way We Live, Love, Parent, and Lead* (New York: Avery Publishing, 2012).

16. Deepak Chopra, *The Seven Spiritual Laws of Success* (San Rafael, CA: Amber-Allen Publishing, 1994).

17. Eckhart Tolle, *A New Earth: Awakening to Your Life's Purpose* (New York: Penguin, 2005).

18. Matt Kahn, *Whatever Arises, Love That: A Love Revolution That Begins with You* (Louisville, CO: Sounds True, 2016).

19. Reena Mukamal, 'Emotional Tears,' *American Academy of Ophthalmology*, 28 February 2017, https://www.aao.org/eye-health/tips-prevention/all-about-emotional-tears.

20. Jill Bolte Taylor. *My Stroke of Insight* (TED Talks), 18 min., 35 sec.; from *TED.com*, https://www.ted.com/talks/jill_bolte_taylor_s_powerful_stroke_of_insight?language=en.

21. Joan Podrazik, 'Dr Brene Brown: Joy is "The Most Terrifying, Difficult Emotion",' *Huffington Post*, 18 March 2013, https://www.huffingtonpost.com/2013/03/18/dr-brene-brown-joy-gratitude-oprah_n_2885983.html.

22. Stephen Levine, *Unattended Sorrow: Recovering from Loss and Reviving the Heart* (Pennsylvania: Rodale Books, 2006).

23. Brené Brown, *Daring Greatly: How the Courage to Be Vulnerable Transforms the Way We Live, Love, Parent, and Lead* (New York: Avery Publishing, 2012).

24. Stephanie Staples, 'Stepping Up—How to Do It and Why It Matters,' *Your Life Unlimited*, http://www.yourlifeunlimited.ca/stepping-up-how-to-do-it-and-why-it-matters/.

25. Pema Chödrön, *Living Beautifully: with Uncertainty and Change* (Colorado: Shambhala Publications, 2012).

26. Therese Tappouni, *The Gifts of Grief: Finding Light in the Darkness of Loss* (Texas: Hierophant Publishing, 2013).

27. Susan L. Smalley and Diana Winston, *Fully Present: The Science, Art, and Practice of Mindfulness,* (Boston: Da Capo Press, 2010).

28. Lynne Twist, *The Soul of Money: Transforming Your Relationship with Money and Life* (New York: W.W. Norton & Company, 2003).

29. Anne D. LeClaire, *Listening Below the Noise: A Meditation on the Practice of Silence* (New York: Harper, 2009).

We hope you enjoyed this Hay House book. If you'd like to receive our online catalog featuring additional information on Hay House books and products, or if you'd like to find out more about the Hay Foundation, please contact:

Hay House, Inc., P.O. Box 5100, Carlsbad, CA 92018-5100
(760) 431-7695 or (800) 654-5126
(760) 431-6948 (fax) or (800) 650-5115 (fax)
www.hayhouse.com® • www.hayfoundation.org

———

Published in Australia by: Hay House Australia Pty. Ltd.,
18/36 Ralph St., Alexandria NSW 2015
Phone: 612-9669-4299 • *Fax:* 612-9669-4144
www.hayhouse.com.au

Published in the United Kingdom by: Hay House UK, Ltd.,
The Sixth Floor, Watson House, 54 Baker Street, London W1U 7BU
Phone: +44 (0)20 3927 7290 • *Fax:* +44 (0)20 3927 7291
www.hayhouse.co.uk

Published in India by: Hay House Publishers India,
Muskaan Complex, Plot No. 3, B-2, Vasant Kunj, New Delhi 110 070
Phone: 91-11-4176-1620 • *Fax:* 91-11-4176-1630
www.hayhouse.co.in

———

Access New Knowledge.
Anytime. Anywhere.

Learn and evolve at your own pace
with the world's leading experts.

www.hayhouseU.com

Free e-newsletters from Hay House, the Ultimate Resource for Inspiration

Be the first to know about Hay House's free downloads, special offers, giveaways, contests, and more!

 Get exclusive excerpts from our latest releases and videos from *Hay House Present Moments*.

 Our *Digital Products Newsletter* is the perfect way to stay up-to-date on our latest discounted eBooks, featured mobile apps, and Live Online and On Demand events.

 Learn with real benefits! *HayHouseU.com* is your source for the most innovative online courses from the world's leading personal growth experts. Be the first to know about new online courses and to receive exclusive discounts.

 Enjoy uplifting personal stories, how-to articles, and healing advice, along with videos and empowering quotes, within *Heal Your Life*.

Sign Up Now!

Get inspired, educate yourself, get a complimentary gift, and share the wisdom!

Visit www.hayhouse.com/newsletters to sign up today!

 HAY HOUSE

HAYHOUSE RADIO
radio for your soul

 HAYHOUSE online learning

Printed in the United States
By Bookmasters